GERMANY

1918-1945

Richard Grunberger

GERMANY
1918 - 1945

B. T. BATSFORD LTD
London

© Richard Grunberger 1964

Printed and bound in Great Britain
by Jarrold and Sons Ltd
London and Norwich for the publishers
B. T. BATSFORD LTD
4 Fitzhardinge Street
London W.1

First published 1964
Reprinted 1966

To H.G.

(1891–1942)

Preface

In preparing this book I have drawn on a wide variety of sources. The bibliography should not be taken as representing the whole of my source-material—but rather as a list of suggestions for further reading. One of my sources must, however, be singled out by name: Bruno Bettelheim's *The Informed Heart*, a work affording anyone who reads it a new and deeper insight into the 'human condition'. In addition I want to express my indebtedness to Mr C. Aronsfeld, Mrs I. Wolff and Mr E. Hearst of the Wiener Library and Mr W. Stanton, Headmaster of the Hasmonean Grammar School.

RICHARD GRUNBERGER

Contents

Acknowledgment

The Author and Publishers wish to thank the following for permission to reproduce illustrations appearing in this book:

C. Bertelsmann Verlag, for permission to base the map on page 30 on a map in *Deutsche Geschichte*, by Michael Freund.

The Cresset Press, for permission to base the maps on pages 54 and 164 on those in *The Rise and Fall of Nazi Germany*, by T. L. Jarman.

London Express News and Feature Services, for permission to reproduce the cartoon by David Low on page 160 from the *Evening Standard* of 21 September 1939.

Hamish Hamilton Ltd, for permission to base the maps on pages 26 and 164 on those in *The Course of German History*, by A. J. P. Taylor.

The Wiener Library Ltd, for permission to reproduce the map on page 168.

The Illustrations

1

The First Reich and After

HITLER INTENDED his description of the Third Reich as the 'Empire that will last a thousand years' to be taken both as a figure of speech and as a forecast whose accuracy would still be borne out ages hence. 'The thousand-year kingdom' is the German metaphor for the millennium of biblical prophecy – and in this sense Hitler projected himself as Germany's Messiah. But in addition the ten centuries of his prediction were also to be interpreted literally, for Hitler was convinced that the Nazi state would hold the world in its thrall quite literally for all time.

Interpreted either way his phrase is an extreme but not untypical example of the hubris which characterised the Nazi mind. And yet there was a mitigating circumstance: in staking his claim to the future continuity of the Third Reich, Hitler had some historical precedent to go on, since ten whole centuries had separated Charlemagne (crowned in AD 800) and Francis II (deposed in 1806), the first and last rulers respectively of the First Reich. This Reich, better known as the 'Holy Roman Empire of the German Nation' (although strictly speaking the last part of this title had only been added by Otto I in 962), had a history stretching back into the mists of the Dark Ages and was thus of impressive antiquity. Who had even heard of Britain, France or Russia at the time of its foundation? An empire of the German nation, at a time when neighbouring peoples had not even properly defined kingdoms of their own!

From this it would appear that in political development the Germans were far ahead of the rest of Europe; but the First Reich in fact throughout most of its existence represented a mythical rather than an actual entity. Effective unity and statehood had been achieved by all major European nations (except the Italians) long before the belated German unification undertaken by Bismarck in 1870–1. The fact that in this matter Germany was theoretically so far ahead, and in reality so far behind the other powers was to have far-reaching consequences both for herself and them.

But before studying the consequences of this retardation we must pay some attention to the causes of Germany's political backwardness, and for this purpose a word-by-word analysis of the First Reich's official title might be as good a starting point as any.

The implication behind *Holy* was the unity-in-duality of Church and State, a medieval ideal of equilibrium invariably contradicted by the actions of Pope or Emperor, or of both.

Roman harked back to the universalism of the empire of the Caesars, who had governed the whole then civilised world; but trying to equate the boundaries of the Reich with those of the whole of Christian civilisation contradicted the limitation implied in the last part of the title—*of the German Nation*—and in addition involved the Emperors in ruinous wars.

Lastly *Empire*. This term at the time implied a supreme authority set above hitherto contending principalities. But 'bastard feudalism' was so much part of the structure of the Reich that when the territorial princes abandoned internecine warfare it was often only for the purpose of jointly defying their Emperor.

To these three debilitating causes of internal weakness must be added a fourth external one. The early development and prosperity of Germany's towns had been based on their situation along medieval Europe's major trade-routes, which led from north Italy across the Alps towards the North Sea coast and the Rhine estuary. The simultaneous discovery of America and of the sea-route to India at the end of the fifteenth century which resulted in the Mediterranean's decline from the world's highway of commerce into a backwater, also meant that the German cities exchanged their focal position along the major overland-routes to one on their periphery. This shift spelt near-disaster to the merchants and burghers of Germany. Stagnation of trade fused with agrarian distress, political discontent, and above all religious ferment to produce the great upheaval of the Protestant Reformation. Since this reformation had been occasioned partly by German resistance to foreign, i.e. Italian, control of the Church and its finances, it might have been expected to further the cause of German national unity. But this was not the case. The north German princes' support of Luther and the Habsburg Emperor's adherence to Rome only tore the deeply-rent Imperial fabric still further. The boundary between the two faiths[1] ran right across Germany, eventually hardening into a barrier which neither missionary zeal, diplomacy nor war could dislodge to any extent.

Whilst continent-wide commitments prevented the Habsburgs from imposing the Catholic Counter-Reformation on the whole of Germany, the Imperial power still sufficed to place bounds on the southward spread of the Lutheran heresy. Although Napoleon liked to speculate what would have happened if Charles V— probably the most powerful Holy Roman Emperor since Charlemagne—had made himself truly head of the German nation by becoming a Protestant, there was never the slightest likelihood of a Habsburg emulating France's Henry IV (as it were in reverse) by forswearing his faith for the sake of national unity.

Thus it was that the Empire eventually became more evenly, and by the same token, more irremediably, divided than any other state affected by the Reformation. There was no conceivable way out of this impasse; the more so since Germany's neighbours, particularly France, had a vested interest in prolonging her internal division and weakness. This was borne out in the course of the Thirty Years War, when power-politics prevented the fires of faith from dying down until the centre of Europe had been turned into a scarred wilderness. From this, her greatest catastrophe, Germany emerged derelict and reduced in population by possibly over a third, as well as irreparably split into a predominantly Catholic south and west and a solidly Protestant north and east.

Whilst most of the Empire was prostrated by war and its aftermath, an 'electorate'[2] in the remote north-east managed to effect a speedy recovery under its Hohenzollern ruler Wilhelm I (1640–88). This 'Great Elector' turned his province into the strongest Protestant state inside the Empire and thereby initiated the remarkable rise of Prussia to German, and subsequently

[1] As defined by the Treaty of Augsburg (1555), which stated that in every province of the Empire the subjects had to embrace their ruler's faith.
[2] One of the eight larger subdivisions of the Empire whose rulers retained the nominal right to elect the Emperor.

European, prominence. The Hohenzollern dynasty and their Junker aristocracy afforded a unique instance of the spirit of Sparta being applied to modern state-building. Prussia was flanked by the hostile but over-extended powers of Sweden and Poland, lacked good soils as well as natural resources and consisted of a motley collection of provinces whose German population had a strong Slav admixture. Gradually advancing from the status of electors to that of kings,[1] the Hohenzollerns welded this disparate entity into a unified whole by rigorous economy, unremitting authoritarian control and ever-present preparedness for, as well as frequent recourse to, war.

The army was so essential a part of the Prussian system that under King Frederick II (1740–86) it absorbed no less than 8,500,000 thalers out of an annual budget of 11,000,000. (This motivated Mirabeau's celebrated quip, 'Whereas elsewhere states have armies, in Prussia the army has a state.') It was small wonder therefore that Frederick felt emboldened to challenge the Imperial power of the Habsburgs when the succession of a woman to the throne (Maria Theresa, 1748–80) seemed to render it specially vulnerable. He wrested the fertile and mineral-rich province of Silesia from Austria's possession and tenaciously clung to his conquest throughout fifteen years of warfare (1740–8 and 1756–63). He subsequently made common cause with the Empress (during the mutually advantageous First Partition of Poland in 1772), but at the very end of his reign he reverted to his earlier policy and challenged the Habsburg power by sponsoring an anti-Austrian League of Princes (1786). Although Frederick the Great died before the League had accomplished very much, this last diplomatic initiative of his still underlined the obvious futility of the Empire's continued existence. What was the purpose of an Imperial authority so moribund that it could be subverted with impunity by the Emperor's nominal vassals?

But before this question could be finally answered, events of far greater import and of bewildering rapidity were beginning to occur beyond the Empire's western borders. The French Revolution had broken out and, though as a source of internal French distraction this event had initially appeared to augur favourably

---

[1] With the Emperor's consent the Elector Frederick III proclaimed himself King Frederick I in 1701.

for France's neighbours, it was soon seen to pose a threat to the governmental and social systems of the whole of Europe. The gravity of this threat for a while even jolted the Austrians and Prussians into taking joint military action against the common enemy (1792). The outcome was far from glorious: the French not only repelled the half-hearted invasion from across the Rhine, but proceeded to commit the world-shaking crime of regicide, and the Prussians unilaterally dropped out of the war the better to be able to participate in the Second and Third Partitions of Poland (1793 and 1795).

Worse was yet to come! In the course of the Revolutionary and Napoleonic wars, the French in turn defeated and greatly reduced in size the states both of the Habsburgs (Austerlitz, 1805), and of the Hohenzollerns (Jena, 1806). Jena represented the very nadir of Prussia's fortunes. The army which under Frederick the Great had withstood the combined might of two European coalitions (1740–8, 1756–63) was annihilated, and Berlin temporarily became Napoleon's headquarters, from which he issued his directives for a continent-wide embargo on Britain's trade. Going beyond the mere reduction of Austria's and Prussia's area, Napoleon further undermined their influence on German affairs by merging a large number of states situated throughout the western part of the Empire into the French-directed Confederation of the Rhine.[1] This meant that henceforth the fate of Germany was to depend on the interplay of forces manipulated not only by Vienna and Berlin, but also by Paris. By thus peremptorily altering the First Reich's internal structure Napoleon had dealt the Empire its long-awaited death-blow; the Holy Roman Emperor accordingly changed his title from that of Francis II of the German Empire into Francis I of Austria (1806).

Whilst France's impact on German affairs in this period was thus quite considerable, Germany's reaction to it was rather contradictory. Along the Rhine, where French control meant among other things the operation of the *Code Napoléon* (freedom of worship, equality before the law, security of property, etc.) in place of the feudal misrule of petty nobles and bishops, the invaders had initially been received as liberators, but had soon

[1] Consisting of Bavaria, Württemberg and over a dozen smaller states along the Rhine.

outstayed their welcome. The rulers of Württemberg, Bavaria and Saxony on the other hand were not averse from continuing to act as French cats-paws throughout the Napoleonic wars in exchange for territorial reward. Prussia by contrast had been left humiliated and bitterly resentful at the peace-terms imposed on her, but the aftermath of Jena turned into the seed-time of a patriotic revival inspired by Stein's political and Scharnhorst's army reforms, as well as by the philosopher Fichte's stirring *Addresses to the German Nation.*

As the scope of Napoleon's continent-wide pretensions, and of his campaigns increased, he exacted ever heavier tribute in the form of taxes, supplies, transport and conscripts from all states under direct and indirect French rule. This caused more and more Germans to look for deliverance from French overlordship and to centre their hopes on a resurgence of Prussia. Napoleon's staggering setback in Russia (1812) gave Prussia the opportunity for wiping out the ignominy of Jena, and from the Battle of Leipzig (1813) to that of Waterloo (1815) the contribution of Prussian arms to allied victory was decisive.

When the leaders of the victorious coalition assembled at the Congress of Vienna to re-shape Europe according to their requirements and the 'status quo ante', they did not contemplate reviving the Holy Roman Empire. This was an indirect tribute to the work of the French, whose centralising and secularising reforms in western Germany it would have been ludicrous to annul for the sake of restoring the chaotic patchwork-quilt arrangements existing previously. By reducing the extreme fragmentation of the Rhenish provinces the French had, for reasons of administrative convenience, brought German unification one step nearer. By substituting the new concept of the nation for that of the dynasty as the focus of men's allegiance they had set an example which peoples as yet without nation-states of their own (such as the Germans and Italians) would one day follow. But their greatest single, although negative, contribution to the growth of German national consciousness had been the experience of a hateful foreign occupation. This humiliating reminder of their own weakness bound many Germans together and made them look to Prussia for leadership. As yet they looked in vain, for although the old Empire was not revived at the Congress of Vienna, the Habsburgs resumed their role of Germanic leadership (for which they were ill-fitted since their Austrian dominions were largely non-German) within the framework of the German Confederation or *Deutsche Bund*. This *Bund* had thirty-odd members, a great improvement upon the 300 diverse units that had constituted the Holy Roman Empire, and as previously Prussia was relegated to a secondary position. Nevertheless, the Hohenzollerns derived the same benefit from their campaigns against France as they had done from earlier ones against Austria, Poland and Sweden: territorial aggrandisement. Under the terms of the Treaty of Vienna they were confirmed in their share of the Partitions of Poland, of which Napoleon had deprived them after Jena, and were awarded part of Saxony as well as the Rhenish province of Westphalia. They would have preferred to annex the whole of neighbouring Protestant Saxony instead of distant, Roman Catholic, and French-influenced Westphalia. But the treaty-makers at Vienna felt that Prussian bayonets along the Rhine ought to help defend Germany against future French aggression. If the Prussian king and his Junker ministers had known in 1815 that their new Rhenish province numbered the Essen iron-master Krupp among its citizens, and contained vast as yet undiscovered mineral deposits in its Ruhr Valley, they might not have expressed such chagrin at the Vienna award.

In 1815, as well as subsequently, the Prussians were thus still more concerned with advancing their narrow state-interests than with fulfilling the all-German aspirations engendered by the 'War of Liberation'. The spirit of the days when von Stein had foreseen Germany's progressive national development towards unity once Napoleon was removed had evaporated. The reasons for Prussia's rejection of the leading role in the movement towards German unity were varied. There was doubtless a great reluctance to challenge the reconstituted Habsburg power, to which nationalism in any form was anathema since it must needs tear the multi-racial Austrian Empire apart. But even more basic than this was the feeling that nationalism was bound up with democracy. In 1815 students at Jena had formed a society (*Burschenschaft*) aiming at both unity and liberty for Germany, and this ran counter to the whole authoritarian structure of the Prussian state where supreme power was wielded, under the king, by the Junkers in their triple function as officers, landowners and local magistrates. In addition there was the fear that an extension of the Prussian state-system to the whole of Germany would lead to its dilution, if not dissolution, a fear exemplified by Prussia's initial aversion to the incorporation of Westphalia.

By 1819 the activities of the Burschenschaften had become such an irritant to the Austrian Chancellor Metternich that on his instigation the Diet of the Germanic Confederation, at its Carlsbad meeting, issued a series of repressive decrees designed to destroy the last vestiges of German political and academic freedom by means of censorship, police surveillance and proscription. Enforcement of the Carlsbad decrees by most members of the Bund accelerated a process of political retrogression, begun at Vienna, that might soon have invited comparison with contemporary Russia, had it not been for far-reaching modifications of the feudal system carried out by von Stein and others during the Napoleonic wars. Whilst German political life thus went into a state of prolonged hibernation from the Carlsbad decrees of 1819 till the Revolution of March 1848, an era known as pre-March or *Vor März*, economically this was a period of change, gradual at first, but gathering ever-increasing momentum subsequently. In 1818 Prussia introduced Maassen's uniform tariff law into all her hitherto disparate provinces from Silesia to Westphalia and thereby created an extensive market unhampered by internal tolls and customs duties. Since such major German rivers as the Rhine, the Elbe and the Oder, in their lower courses all flowed through her territory, Prussia was now in a strong position for suggesting an extension of her own tariff arrangements to most of the rest of Germany. The suggested Customs Union, or *Zollverein*, on Prussian terms did not at first commend itself to many members of the Bund. Some states even proceeded to establish their own miniature rival 'Common Markets', for example, Bavaria and Württemberg in 1828. But by 1834 this South-Western Union decided to discontinue its separate existence and to merge economically with Prussia, and by 1842 among the larger states only Austria and Hanover were still outside the Zollverein. In the previous year the Prussian economist F. List had stated in his *National System of Political Economy* that the national state is the natural unit of economic production, and had stressed the need for high tariffs as a means of fostering Germany's industries. Since the achievement of the national state was a liberal demand, List's insistence on high tariffs shows an important divergence from contemporary English thinking where such Liberal spokesmen as Gladstone and Cobden made Free Trade the chief plank of their platform. The pulling-down of most of Germany's internal tariff barriers was followed by a rapid extension of the railway system. Of this the historian Treitschke was to write later, 'The railways completed the work of the Zollverein and shook the nation out of its state of commercial stagnation. Because of them life had assumed a different aspect in the 1840s.'

That decade also showed a different aspect as far as German politics were concerned. The Burschenschaften and the Liberals had been encouraged by the Paris Revolution of 1830, and the subsequent Polish revolt against the Tsar, to carry out sporadic uprisings, especially in south-western Germany, where one or two rulers had granted constitutions to their subjects. It is a matter of interest that the Hambach Festival of 1832, held under the black-red-gold banner of German Liberal Nationalism, was also attended by French and Polish revolutionaries. The reception accorded to these foreign fighters for liberty showed that inter-nationalism was a prominent feature of the German unification movement in its early phase.

After Hambach the country as a whole relapsed into the political torpor so congenial to Metternich as well as to the great majority of the heads of the individual states, although there were rumblings of protest when one of the latter, the Elector of Hanover, saw fit to dismiss a number of outstanding academics from their university chairs in the course of a constitutional squabble. Two significant events occurred in 1840: a new King, Frederick William IV (1840–58), ascended the Prussian throne, and the French, casting around for a diversion from their Middle Eastern set-back at the hands of Palmerston, seemed to be making threatening noises across the Rhine. This led to an upsurge of patriotic feeling reminiscent of 1813. Once again German patriots looked to Prussia which was mounting 'The Watch on the Rhine' (in the words of the song composed at that time), and which seemed by a variety of factors predestined to leadership of the whole nation. She stood guard not only on the Rhine against the French, but also along the

Vistula against the Slavs. She possessed in her Westphalian and Silesian coalfields the greatest mineral potential of the whole Bund and was now ruled over by a king who reputedly sympathised with the national cause.

The French scare of 1840 soon passed but the new King of Prussia justified some of the hopes initially placed in him when he allowed such previously victimised nationalists as the brothers Grimm—of fairytale fame—to be restored to their university chairs, and when he appointed 'patriots' to important positions. In 1847 Frederick William IV raised liberal hopes still further by setting up a Central Diet[1] for the whole of Prussia (in place of the local diets which had hitherto functioned in the various provinces), only to dash them again when he ruled out any likelihood of his ever being prepared to grant a constitution to the Prussian people.

Early in 1848 Paris became the centre of a political earthquake for the third time in sixty years, but in this Year of Revolutions its tremors spread over most of the Continent within a matter of days. The long 'Pre-March' of Metternich's rule over the Confederation was abruptly terminated almost as soon as the news from Paris had reached Vienna. All at once the frontier barriers between the individual German states appeared to be so much matchwood, to be blown away by the storm of the national revolution. Princes who had hitherto ruled by the 'Grace of God' tacked furiously with the wind, hurriedly amending this phrase to read 'by the Grace of the People', and remounted their shaky thrones as constitutional instead of absolute rulers.

In an atmosphere of enthusiastic expectancy an all-German Parliament, the first in history, met at Frankfurt. Its initial major concern was the drawing up of a constitution as the legal framework around which the new state of a free and united Germany could be created. The delegates dutifully discharged this primary task, but their 'near perfect' constitution was to remain a dead letter. Free, united Germany was stillborn, lacking a breath of life stronger than that which wafted out of the debating chambers of the Frankfurt Parliament.

Among the many and complex reasons for the failure of the German 1848 Revolution, first place should be accorded to

---

[1] This was based on a three-class franchise with the very rich, the middle-income and the low-income groups all having equal representation.

Austria's anomalous position as a Germanic power. Only 6,000,000 out of the Habsburgs' 36,000,000 subjects were German,[1] and of the great non-German majority the various Slav races (Czechs, Slovenes, Croats, etc.) formed the most numerous, though hitherto least powerful, group.

The Frankfurt parliamentarians had invited representatives of Bohemia to join in their deliberations, although that province was far from purely German, but they expected the Czech peasants to follow the lead of the German town-dwellers as a matter of course. There was, therefore, great consternation at Frankfurt when the Czech leader Palacky not only declined the invitation, but proceeded subsequently to convene a separate all-Slav Congress at Prague. To Slav eyes the stagnant and illiberal Habsburg Empire seemed a more trustworthy guarantor of their future than alliance with the cause of German nationalism.

But while the Emperor's Slav subjects would not join the new state, his German ones could not. The loyalty of their army had enabled the Habsburgs to maintain their Empire intact despite a number of nationalist insurrections and the new Emperor, Francis Joseph (1848–1916), firmly set his face against the union of Austria with Germany, the concept of *Grossdeutschland* (Greater Germany) advocated at Frankfurt.

There still remained the possibility of *Kleindeutschland* (Little Germany), the fusion into one unit of the Confederation's remaining thirty-eight members. Among them Prussia was by far the strongest. Like Austria she was part German and part Slav, but the proportion was reversed: as against 14,000,000 Germans there were 2,000,000 Poles in the Hohenzollern state. Even so, the Polish problem was to bedevil the work of the Frankfurt Assembly. The Poles of Posen province had complained of ill-treatment at the hands of the Prussian authorities, thereby confronting the German Parliament with an agonising choice between the professed principles of the 1848 Revolution (liberty and equality for all peoples) and support for Prussia on whom its hope for all-German leadership rested. In this conflict between liberalism and 'healthy national egotism' (to quote Wilhelm Jordan, one of the Assembly's leaders), the latter easily triumphed. Having listened

---

[1] Their area of settlement consisted of the Alpine provinces of Austria and parts of Bohemia.

to Jordan's statement that German conquests in Poland were a natural necessity and that 'the law of history does not resemble that of the legal code', the Frankfurt Parliament decided to ratify the actions already taken by the Prussians against their helpless Polish minority. But Frankfurt's regard for the interests of Prussia was not reciprocated. In the early stages of the Revolution (March 1848), King Frederick William IV had caused nation-wide rejoicing by his declaration, 'I place myself and my people under the honour-worthy banner of the German Reich. Prussia will merge itself into Germany forthwith.' Yet when the revolutionary tide was ebbing and the Germans of Schleswig-Holstein were appealing for their compatriots' support against Danish annexation, the Prussian King ignored Frankfurt's urgent entreaties and did little to help them. He was more concerned about the possible objections of Britain and Russia to drastic changes along the entrance to the Baltic than with furthering the cause of national Germany.

Lacking both an army of its own and the courage to mobilise the civilian population, the Assembly gradually declined into an impotent debating society. But then, after some months of further deliberations, it hit on an apparent way out of its difficulties by offering the all-German crown to the King of Prussia. A deputation was sent from Frankfurt to Berlin; it asked Frederick William IV to accede to the demands of the German people by becoming their Emperor. Yet the King's scant sympathy for constitutional monarchy was mingled with a healthy respect for the Austrian Empire; he knew that the Habsburgs would be unlikely to accept the Little German solution any more willingly than the Greater German one, since it would involve their exclusion from German affairs.

He accordingly turned down the proffered all-German crown with the explanation that he would accept it from his fellow princes, but not from popular representatives: 'I shall not stoop to pick up a crown from the gutter' (April 1849). This reply left the already deeply divided Frankfurt parliamentarians completely hamstrung. When in addition Frederick William IV ordered the withdrawal of Prussia's delegates, the Assembly's days were numbered. It moved to Stuttgart only to be dispersed by the Duke of Württemberg's troops. This left just one area in all Germany where the democratic principles of Frankfurt still prevailed: the south-western province of Baden. And soon, the same Prussian army that had earlier on ignored the Assembly's plea for military support of Schleswig-Holstein, invaded Baden to extinguish the last flicker of the spirit of 1848.

The great German-Jewish poet Heinrich Heine wrote a fitting epitaph on the events of 1848–9. 'Revolution is a misfortune, but an even greater misfortune is a revolution that miscarries.' (Heine spent most of his adult life in self-imposed exile in the country of more successful revolutions—France.)

But even though Germany's 1848 Revolution had miscarried, the return to a complete 'status quo ante' was somewhat delayed. In 1850 the Prussian King granted his subjects a constitution; feeling the need for some sort of gesture in the direction of greater national unity, he also mooted the creation of the nucleus of united Germany in the form of a union between his own and some neighbouring states. This project was instantly vetoed by Austria and Frederick William IV had to submit to Metternich's successor, Schwarzenberg, under humiliating circumstances (Punctuation of Olmütz).

The old Confederation was revived unaltered; the Austrian Emperor, as in 1815, was not only its most powerful ruler, but apparently more powerful than all the others combined. Yet subsequent events were to prove that Austria was neither as strong, nor Prussia as weak, as they had seemed at Olmütz. During the 1850s and 60s industrialisation proceeded at an increasing pace in the coal and iron-rich provinces of Westphalia and Silesia. Prussia's stock was not only rising in the economic field. The fact that she now at long last had a constitution as well as a parliament, although neither was fully democratic, made her stand out among other states of the Confederation. This trend became still more pronounced after the accession in 1858 of Wilhelm I, a king holding a sincere belief in Prussia's German mission and evincing an outward respect for constitutionalism in marked contrast to his predecessor's, 'I shall not allow a scrap of paper to come between me and Divine Providence'. It should be added, however, that Wilhelm at heart also favoured the divinely-inspired theory of monarchy, but he realised the need to move with the times.

Wilhelm I's outward respect for constitutional issues involved

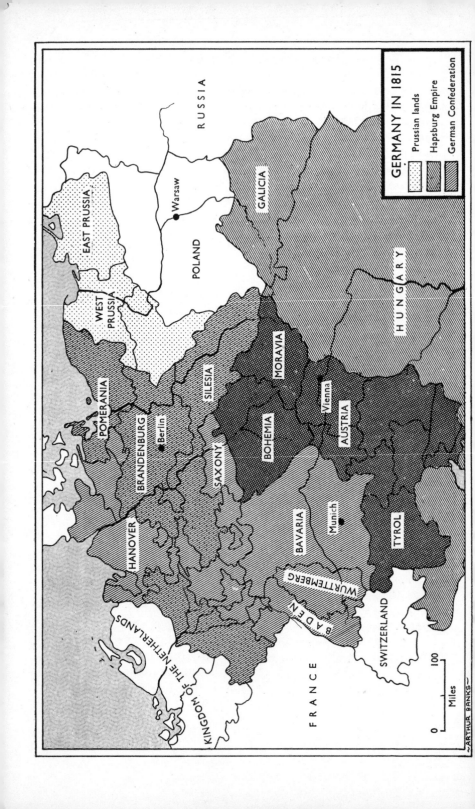

him in a political crisis within three years of his accession. His military advisers wanted to expand the effective strength of the army so as to keep pace with the continuous increase in population. This required additional taxes which the Prussian Parliament refused to vote until the government had fulfilled certain conditions. The real issue at stake was whether it was ultimately the generals or the elected representative of the people who exercised control over the army. Constitutional deadlock threatened when neither side showed any inclination to give way over the Army Reforms. Both in Parliament and the country was there a solid majority against the Junkers of the General Staff. Failing to discern any possible way out of the stalemate the King even thought of abdicating, but he was spared this extremity by the timely advice of the War Minister, von Roon, 'All that is required to solve the constitutional deadlock is the appointment of a strong man as Chancellor'.

The strong man suggested by von Roon was Otto von Bismarck, who soon after his appointment to the highest office of state thus outlined his own approach to constitutional problems: 'Germany is not interested in Prussia's liberalism, but in her might. The great questions of the day will not be decided by speeches and majority resolutions, but by blood and iron.' It was in this uncomplicated manner that the new Chancellor immediately proceeded to deal with the particular issue of the disputed army reforms. The government stuck to its guns both metaphorically and literally; tax inspectors collected the illegally increased taxes and from this additional revenue new regiments were equipped in conformity with von Roon's specifications. Parliament was now confronted with the grim alternative of either calling on the people to resist the tax-officials or of accepting Bismark's illegalities as accomplished facts it was powerless to do anything about. Resistance might involve bloodshed and civil war, whereas submission would speedily reduce the Diet in Berlin to a mere talking-shop.

England's Long Parliament in 1642, the American Colonists' Convention in 1776, and the French National Assembly in 1789, had all decided to take the perilous path of resistance to established authority, but Prussia's parliamentarians in 1862 were men of rather different mettle. Whilst continuing their protestations they shrank from issuing what in the last resort might have amounted to a call to insurrection, and submitted, still registering their outraged protests.

This first, and rather cheap, victory of Bismarck's over his opponents at home was soon eclipsed by signal success abroad. He settled once and for all the question of the two Duchies which had been in abeyance since the fiasco of 1848. Prussia's unconstitutionally expanded forces attacked and defeated Denmark (1864) and Schleswig and Holstein were successively annexed by Prussia.

Another lightning campaign in 1866 solved the tangled problem of Austria's relationship with the other states of the Bund which had been a drag on Germany's progress for so long. The battle of Sadowa was a triumph for Bismarck's diplomacy and Moltke's strategy. It resulted in Austria's exclusion from further interference in German affairs, and a Prussian-dominated North German Confederation took the place of the Habsburg-directed Deutsche Bund. (In addition the incorporation of Hanover gave Prussia a continuous belt of territory stretching from the French frontier to that with Russia.) These astounding successes were held in retrospect to justify the breaches of the constitution perpetrated by the Chancellor ever since taking office. The Prussian Parliament accordingly by a three-to-one majority voted Bismarck an indemnity for the previous four years' illegal collection of taxes. In other words the Liberal MPs ruefully admitted to having been wrong all along in opposing a policy which had culminated in such notable advances of Prussian power. Thus was created the dangerous precedent for judging a policy by the standards not of right but of might—a tendency that was to influence Germany's subsequent history to a disturbing extent.

2

The Second Reich

THE GREATEST SINGLE SUCCESS of his career awaited Bismarck when four years later Napoleon III allowed a complacent France to blunder into war with Prussia (1870–1). To many Germans France was a potent symbol of their own country's past weakness— Louis XIV's devastation of the Palatinate had been as little forgotten as the first Napoleon's successful (and his nephew's pathetically ineffective) designs on Germany's integrity. Every victory of Moltke's superb fighting machine over the 'hereditary enemy' therefore still further strengthened the iron hoops of friendship with which Bismarck was binding the rest of Germany to Prussia. As Prussia's armies progressed inexorably towards Paris, she herself advanced into the front rank of the powers of Europe.

At the Hall of Mirrors in Louis XIV's Palace of Versailles was enacted the greatest scene in German history since the coronation of Charlemagne: the proclamation of the Second Reich, a super-state to be ruled over by Wilhelm I of Prussia as Emperor of all Germans (except those in the Habsburg dominions). Germany was at last united, not in defiance of her illiberal princes, but under their leadership. By the decision not of majorities, but of the God of Battles, had Frederick William IV's stipulation of 1849 been fulfilled. The all-German crown had been offered to Wilhelm I by his fellow princes and not by the representatives of the German people, although the latter had also made their presence un-mistakably felt at Metz and Sedan.

The new constitution of 1871 was only an extension of Bismarck's arrangements for the North German Confederation to the whole of the Reich. Its preamble significantly stated that the constitution

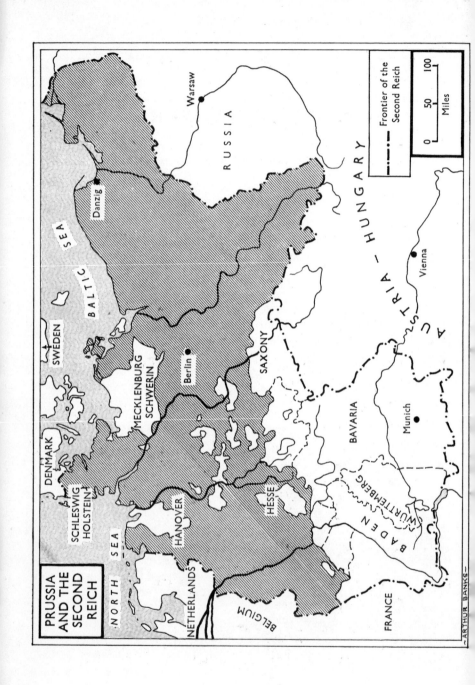

PRUSSIA
AND THE
SECOND
REICH

Frontier of the
Second Reich

0   50   100
Miles

NORTH SEA

BALTIC SEA

SWEDEN

DENMARK

SCHLESWIG
HOLSTEIN

MECKLENBURG
SCHWERIN

HANOVER

NETHERLANDS

BELGIUM

HESSE

WÜRTEMBERG

BADEN

FRANCE

BAVARIA

Munich

SAXONY

Berlin

Danzig

RUSSIA

Warsaw

AUSTRIA - HUNGARY

Vienna

~ARTHUR BANKS~

took the form of a grant by the various rulers of the Germanic states to their subjects—an indication that political initiative inside the Empire was to flow from above and not below. And yet superficially the Second Reich resembled a constitutional monarchy in many of its aspects. The parliament (*Reichstag*) had wide legislative and budgetary powers and was elected on the basis of universal franchise, whereas in Britain at this time the right to vote was still hedged around with residential and property qualifications.

But in substance Bismarck's Empire represented the inversion of Frederick William IV's dictum about Prussia henceforth merging into Germany, since what happened in 1871 was, in fact, the merging of Germany into Prussia. For although the German legislature had the power to make laws and grant supplies it did not control the executive which basically consisted of one man: the Minister-President of Prussia, who was automatically Chancellor of the whole Reich. It was in the method of selecting this Chancellor, the keystone of the Bismarckian edifice, that the democratic process was most clearly seen to be honoured only in the breach. The continued operation of Prussia's three-class franchise ensured that her government was not genuinely representative, whilst the constitutional clause vesting the power of appointing or dismissing the Chancellor solely in the Emperor meant that the Reich government, whilst representative, was not 'responsible' (i.e. responsible to, and therefore controlled by Parliament). Beside the Chancellor the main pillar of Imperial authority was the army of the Reich, which again was mainly an extension of that of Prussia. But since for centuries past the various German states had led a separate existence and their inhabitants had strong provincial loyalties (especially in Catholic Bavaria), Prussia's political and military dominance inside the new Reich was to a not insignificant extent counter-balanced by the continued internal autonomy of the states. Bavaria, for instance, not only retained its own royal dynasty, the Wittelsbachs, but also maintained its separate army.

The whole system had been designed as a complex structure embodying mutually contradictory features of democracy and authoritarian rule, of 'state-rights' and centralisation. Its pivotal point was the Chancellorship whose occupant in turn depended first and foremost on the support of the Emperor, but to some extent also on that of the electorate.

Bismarck, the first Chancellor, was at all times assured of the support of Kaiser Wilhelm I. His relationship with the electorate was not as clear-cut. Although he consistently attracted the support of Conservatives, since he was a fellow Junker, and of National Liberals, since he had unified Germany, his relationship with the Catholic Centre party was characterised by intermittent, and with the working-class Social Democrats, by permanent hostility. Internally the first decade of Bismarck's Chancellorship was taken up by a prolonged and indecisive struggle against the Catholic Church (known as the *Kulturkampf*), and the second by his equally —as subsequent events were to prove—ineffective attempt at containing the advance of the German Labour movement. An important turning-point was the year 1879 when he patched up a compromise peace with the Catholics to secure his flank before launching an all-out anti-Socialist campaign. In this year he also made the German economy revert from Free Trade to a fully-fledged protectionism. Although high tariffs were injurious to the interests of the German consumers, they were a boon to the Conservative agrarians and the National Liberal industrialists, since they protected them from the competition of cheap foreign (largely American) grain and cheap foreign (mainly British) manufactures. It should be added that a minority of National Liberals put so high a premium on their attachment to Free Trade that they formed a break-away Left National Liberal Party.

Among this multiplicity of parties Bismarck maintained a position of aloof balance, for although his measures, such as the return to protection, might serve certain vested interests, he did not want to see the Chancellorship, and with it the lofty Imperial authority, dragged into the dust of party politics. In fact the post-1879 tariffs enabled him to reduce the scope of party political activity, since annually increasing revenue from customs would make him more independent of budgetary control exercised by the Reichstag. This growth of revenue also helped the German government to launch its great pioneering scheme of workers' accident, pension and health insurance (1881-9), designed to wean the proletariat away from Social Democracy—a 'welfare-state' carrot to complement the stick of the repressive anti-Socialist laws. When popular support threatened to desert him at times Bismarck skilfully re-established himself by inflating French war-scares or attributing anarchistic attempts on the Emperor's life to the Social Democrats.

The 'Socialist peril' was in effect a paradoxical tribute to the Reich's economic advance under Bismarck's rule. Stimulated by the incorporation of Alsace-Lorraine and the payment of the £200,000,000 French indemnity, German industry had boomed in the early 1870s, when within three years as many iron and steel plants had been set up in Prussia as in the whole preceding three-quarter century. This phenomenal growth was interrupted by a stock exchange crash in 1873 (which antisemites blamed on to Jewish manipulation of the market) but it continued subsequently, although at a reduced rate of increase brought about by the periodic recurrence of declines in trade. The industrialists, who understandably wanted to be safeguarded against such setbacks, pressed the government to embark on a programme of colonisation. (At the time of 'the scramble for Africa' overseas possessions were universally coveted as profitable outlets and raw material sources for the national economy.) Industrialists and explorers sponsored the formation of a German Colonial Society. Soon, the African exploits of such pioneer Empire-builders as Lüderitz and Nachtigall fired the imagination of a public increasingly determined not to be excluded by Britain and France from sharing in the partition of the Dark Continent. Bismarck eventually had to give way to rising popular clamour. And so it came about that the man who, ever since 1871, had declared Germany a sated power desiring no further expansion, and who in 1878 had presided over the Berlin Congress as an 'honest broker', interested only in maintaining European stability and the continued isolation of France, took steps, which from 1884 onwards, resulted in Germany acquiring a sizeable colonial empire. South-West Africa, Cameroons, Togo and Tanganyika, as well as various Pacific islands, were all brought under the black-white-red Imperial flag within a short while, giving the Reich 12,000,000 coloured subjects and an increase in area of 1,000,000 square miles. This soothed nationalist passions to an extent, though the expected economic benefits did not materialise, and by 1913 the colonies accounted for precisely ½ per cent of Germany's total trade.

Bismarck's reluctance to acquire colonies was partly motivated by his wish not to antagonise Britain whose goodwill (next to that of Russia), he considered essential for his design of keeping France diplomatically isolated and thus incapable of launching a war of revenge for 1871. But since Germany now had a colonial empire, the necessity of expanding her naval potential could not be overlooked. In 1887 work was started on the Kiel Canal, with a view to creating speedy communication between Germany's North Sea and Baltic coasts, and within two years Britain showed herself alive to the potentialities of this trend by legislating that the Royal Navy's strength should henceforth equal that of any other two fleets combined (Salisbury's Naval Defence Act, 1889). This, in turn, caused many Germans to complain, 'We are often charged with militarism; what about British navalism?'

In the interim Wilhelm I had died (1888). The old Emperor had allowed himself to be guided by Bismarck ever since the latter's assumption of control in Prussia—the best part of three decades. This untroubled relationship between the respective heads of state and government was, however, brought to a sudden end soon after the next effective Emperor, Wilhelm II, had ascended the throne. The new Kaiser was no more than 29 years old, but he was both self-willed and bursting with energy. Firmly convinced that he knew what was best for the country, he decided in 1890 that he could henceforth do without the advice of the aged Chancellor, who had possibly been the most successful, if hardly the most moral, statesman of his century. By an odd paradox the 'pilot' had himself facilitated his 'being dropped' in such a cavalier fashion through his own undemocratic constitutional device of 1871 whereby the power to appoint or dismiss the Chancellor had been vested solely in the Emperor.

Among crucial points at issue between the old pilot and the new captain was Bismarck's over-cautious approach to Germany's colonial and naval expansion. Wilhelm II also glibly rejected the Chancellor's traditional policy of trying to maintain a special relationship with the two mutually antagonistic powers of Russia and Austria-Hungary for fear of either becoming an ally of France. Although Bismarck had, in fact, drawn closer to Austria, which power could be more easily managed than the Slav colossus (both on account of size and common traditions), he had specifically attempted to guard against a widening of the breach with Russia by concluding a special Reinsurance Treaty with her, which had to be renewed periodically. Wilhelm II considered this diplomatic safeguard superfluous and allowed it to lapse in 1890.

He also had a different approach to internal German questions. Since neither Bismarck's stick nor his carrot had accomplished the object of stunting the growth of the Social Democrats, the Kaiser saw the need for some drastic re-thinking of the problem. His own enthusiastic, but decidedly short-term, solution consisted of somehow creating for himself the image of a People's Emperor who would command the affection of the proletariat without recourse either to threats or bribes. In short, Wilhelm II was brimming over with many novel ideas, for none of which he was indebted to Bismarck. These ideas were often so self-contradictory that they caused a foreign diplomat to describe the Kaiser thus: 'In him, as in Hamlet, there exist the germs of various men and we cannot foresee which of them will prevail; or whether when one has finally developed he will amaze us by his greatness or by his triviality.'

The emphasis during the first years of the new reign was very much on greatness. The beginning of the Kaiser's personal rule—personal, since none of the successive chancellors could at first aspire to Bismarck's massive authority and influence—coincided with the foundation of yet another patriotic organisation, the All-German League. Its sponsors included leading industrialists; the subsequently highly influential press-magnate Hugenberg was a co-founder. The League's chief aim was the creation of a state comprising all Nordic peoples, implying incorporation within the Reich not merely of the German-speaking Austrians and Swiss, but of the Dutch, the Flemings, the Scandinavians, etc. Since there were substantial German minorities in Eastern Europe as well as North and South America, the obvious inference to be drawn was that the Reich projected by the all-Germans would eventually extend over most of Europe, if not the world.

A patriotic association with more practical aims was the German Navy League, founded in 1898 under the patronage of Grand Admiral von Tirpitz. These German 'navalists', who enjoyed financial support from big firms eager for government contracts, wanted to make the German public conscious of the need for a High Seas fleet which would be capable of executing *Weltpolitik* (a world-wide policy). With this the Kaiser was in full agreement. 'Germany's destiny lies on the High Seas' had almost become his personal motto. The Kiel Canal was opened in 1895; three years later the Reichstag approved Tirpitz's Greater Navy Bill which initiated a vast expansion of the German fleet. Subsequent bills had the ambitious aims of enabling Germany to compete with Britain in naval tonnage and armaments. Although parity in these fields was never to be achieved, the resulting arms race, with its emphasis on feverish dreadnought construction, contributed markedly to the war-psychosis then beginning to grip Europe.

In 1900 the Reich was afforded an opportunity for Weltpolitik on a moderate scale when the suppression of the anti-European Boxer Rebellion in China necessitated the dispatch of German military units to the Far East. Addressing them prior to embarkation, the Kaiser laid down the following rules in his Order of the Day: 'No pardon is to be given—prisoners will not be taken. Use your arms so that for a thousand years no Chinese will dare look askance at a German. . . .'

On visits to Turkey (1898) and to Morocco (1905) Wilhelm II struck a more ambitious note in Weltpolitik by calling on all Muslims to look upon the Reich as their protector—an appeal which had obvious anti-French and anti-British overtones. The Hamlet aspect of the Kaiser's character was revealed when the author of the 1895 Kruger telegram (congratulating the Boer President on having foiled the British-inspired Jameson raid), stated in 1908: 'I'm pro-British; at the time of Britain's initial reverses in the Boer War, I worked out a plan of campaign, similar to the one later adopted by Lord Roberts, which I forwarded to London. I also refused to join Russia and France in an anti-British front at that time.' (Interview published in the *Daily Telegraph*.)

The possibility of joint Russo-French action would never have existed in the Bismarck era; it was Wilhelm II's deliberate failure to renew the Reinsurance Treaty with the Tsar that had given France the opportunity of ending her isolation. Henceforth the alliance between Russia and France was to be one of the two constant factors in the European situation: the other being the Bismarck-inspired combination of Germany, Austria and Italy. The position of such previously non-aligned powers as Britain and

Turkey became more clearly defined after the turn of the century. Great Britain, apprehensive of German naval, colonial and trade rivalry, concluded the *Entente Cordiale* with France in 1904, and an agreement with Russia in 1907, whereas Turkey came more and more under German influence, with the Sultan's government granting wide concessions to the promoters of the Berlin-Baghdad railway from 1903 onwards.

This line-up of the great powers set the scene for a succession of crises in which each side dared the other to go to war over some deliberately inflamed issue, or to give way and lose face. In the First Moroccan Crisis (1905) Germany had the satisfaction of enforcing the dismissal of the French Foreign Minister Delcassé, one of the architects of the Entente Cordiale. She scored another success in 1908 when she menacingly warned Russia off supporting Serbia against the Austrians who had permanently annexed Serb-speaking Bosnia.

This was Weltpolitik on a grand scale, even if (as will presently be seen) its successes were rather short-lived. But these successes had not cost the Reich a single drop of blood, a circumstance possibly attributable to its abundant possession of iron. By the beginning of the twentieth century Germany's annual production of iron and steel was exceeding that of Great Britain, formerly the workshop of the world. The Reich's electrical industry, the fastest-growing sector in a country-wide proliferation of manufacture, accounted for half the world's trade in electrical products by 1913. In part this vast output had also been stimulated by an acceleration of the armaments programme for which the Reichstag voted ever larger appropriations. By 1910 the Reich's arms potential amounted to two-thirds of the combined Anglo-French military strength. In the following year the German Chief of Staff, General von Schlieffen died after devoting the last ten years of his life to the task of working out a foolproof plan for the rapid capture of Paris in a future war. At about the same time, the Second Moroccan Crisis broke over a distracted continent. But on this occasion it was France which managed, with the backing of its allies, to compel a German retreat. Morocco with its valuable mineral resources, passed into the French zone of influence. War had been brought one step nearer.

In 1912 the British Secretary of War, Haldane, visited Berlin in the hope of reducing tension between the two countries, but his mission was as devoid of success as had been earlier ones undertaken by Joseph Chamberlain and by McKenna. From the vantage-point of Berlin the *entente* of Britain, France and Russia, which had just carried the day over the Moroccan issue, appeared as a conspiracy aiming at the encirclement of the Reich. Nor was there any way of removing the greatest single irritant in Anglo-German relations by calling a halt to the naval race since Germany's demand for naval parity, i.e. equality of tonnage and armament, could not be reconciled with Britain's insistence on the 'double-standard'.

In a very popular book published at this time, *Germany and the Next War*, the author, General Bernhardi, argued that the alternative facing the Reich at this stage of its development was either 'world power or destruction'. The All-German League's programme of the same period proposed the following measures for the internal strengthening of the Second Empire: compulsory Germanisation or expulsion of the Polish, Danish and French minorities living inside the Reich's boundaries; the banning of all Socialist-engineered strikes; the denial of voting-rights to women (since 'a woman's greatest strength lies in her instincts'); the establishment of a strong authority capable of giving a firm lead to the nation and the withdrawal of citizenship rights from all Jews living in the Reich.

The All-Germans' compulsory Germanisation proposals were a reminder of the fact that Bismarck's internal colonisation programme in the eastern provinces (in 1886 the Reichstag had voted 100,000,000 marks for buying out Polish farmers and replacing them by Germans) had been unsuccessful. The Poles' tenacious retention of their farms affronted nationalist Germans doubly since it meant that compact alien minorities continued to exist inside the Reich, and that Germany's large annual population surplus could not be channelled back to the land; the resultant loss of German manpower through emigration was quite considerable, amounting to well over a million during the reign of Kaiser Wilhelm I.

Gradually, however, Germany's industrial expansion absorbed more and more of her population increase and the need for emigration no longer arose. Population had about trebled in a hundred years, rising from 24,000,000 in 1815 to 67,000,000 in 1914; the national income had practically doubled in less than 20 years, to stand at 43,000,000,000 marks in 1913 as against 23,000,000,000 in 1896. These staggering increases were accompanied by rapid urbanisation—the proportion of town-dwellers had shot up from a few per cent to three-fifths of the total population within two generations. As most of the new town-dwellers were of course industrial workers, this had given rise to an intensification of the 'social question'—hence the All-Germans' proposal for outlawing strikes.

Nineteen-thirteen was a year of increased preparedness for war. The special importance of the army in German public life was demonstrated by the 'Zabern affair', so called after a garrison town in Alsace where the military had unlawfully arrested a number of civilians. When a large majority in the Reichstag voted that the local commander be brought to trial, an army court-martial not only cleared him completely, but he was soon afterwards made the recipient of a high military decoration. The same year saw the widening of the Kiel Canal to facilitate the passage of dread-noughts and the imposition of a capital levy of 1,000,000,000 marks for additional arms expenditure. The Reichstag had passed these measures against the votes of the Socialists who had emerged from the 1912 elections as the strongest single party in the country. This apparent strength of a party consistently opposing the arms race and pledged to socialist internationalism, was a source of comfort to peace-lovers everywhere, who by now were deeply disturbed by the drift towards war.

The crisis broke early next summer when the heir to the Austrian throne was assassinated by a Serb patriot on 28 June 1914. The events subsequent upon this latest Balkans[1] outrage were a delayed reaction to developments during the Bosnian crisis of 1908. Russia was this time determined not to suffer the humiliations of six years earlier and fully backed the Serbs against the peremptory demands of the Austrians. The Reich, which had originally pledged Austria its support for a localised war in the Balkans, felt compelled to operate the Schlieffen Plan to counteract Russia's order for general mobilisation. War against France followed automatically and Britain was drawn into the conflict when the German

[1] Only recently the theatre of two successive, but localised, wars.

army, conforming to Schlieffen's strategic design, invaded neutral Belgium as a first step towards the rapid capture of Paris.

Here at last was the strong leadership the All-Germans had been demanding. The German people's response to it was immediate and practically unanimous. The Socialist deputies joined the rest of the Reichstag in voting war credits, thus lending substance to Wilhelm II's 'In war all politics cease; henceforth I acknowledge no parties, only Germans'. Outbursts of patriotic enthusiasm swept the country, strangers embraced each other in the street, rich and poor fraternised. They saw the war as a just crusade against the enemies encircling Germany, enemies whom they confidently expected to be struck down one by one. The fall of Paris and end of French resistance within six weeks, the eastward transfer of the army immediately afterwards to annihilate the slow-moving forces of the Tsar, presenting a German-dominated Continent as a *fait accompli* to the British before they had fully mobilised their resources: these were the predictions on which both the General Staff and the German man in the street based their anticipation of early victory.

The fulfilment of their hopes hinged on the successful execution of the Schlieffen Plan. The General's dying words had been: 'Don't forget to strengthen the right flank'. But it was this very mistake which the new Chief of Staff, von Moltke (junior), committed out of fear of denuding the left flank, in the direction of which he expected a French counter-attack. The envisaged lightning advance was in consequence slowed down and was finally brought to a standstill along the Marne, falling a few, but crucially decisive, miles short of its objective: Paris. A contributory factor to this confounding of Germany's deep-seated certainty of early victory had been the unexpectedly swift mobilisation of the Tsar's vast but ill-equipped forces. A sudden Russian incursion into East Prussia necessitated switching troops from the western front, and although General von Hindenburg, hastily recalled from retirement, gained a great victory—and his countrymen's undying affection—at Tannenberg, the Russian defeat in the east had helped to deny Germany victory in the west.

The swift campaigns planned by the Reich's General Staff now gradually gave way to a long-drawn-out war of attrition against the Anglo-French in Flanders and elsewhere. For some time neither side possessed sufficient strength to gain a decisive advantage over the other, and adjustments of the front-line often involved casualty figures higher than those incurred throughout whole wars earlier in history.

From the very commencement of hostilities the German High Command had usurped the functions of the civilian government and assumed control over every aspect of the nation's life. It was on the Generals' instruction that Chancellor Bethmann-Hollweg presented the ultimatum to Belgium that brought Britain into the war. The Chancellor had tried to justify the violation of Belgian neutrality in a Reichstag speech carrying remarkably little conviction, although German public opinion did not long have to trouble itself on that score, since a statement by ninety-three eminent artists and scientists in 1915 exonerated the Reich from all blame for the plight of Belgium, responsibility for which was laid at the door of the war-mongering Entente.

In February 1916 plans were mooted for an unrestricted submarine campaign against Allied shipping which would cut Britain off from her essential overseas supplies and make her drop out of the war. Bethmann-Hollweg opposed this, but the subsequent appointment of Hindenburg, assisted by his Quarter-master, General Ludendorff, to supreme military command in August, and the Entente's lack of responsiveness to the American President Wilson's peace-feelers in December 1916, led to the Chancellor being overruled. The U-boat campaign was launched, only to boomerang on the heads of its instigators when the sinking of the *Lusitania* brought the United States into the war on the Allied side (April 1917). But since America's mobilisation and transportation of her troops was bound to be a slow process, the German High Command felt it could base its strategy on such reassuring developments in the Allied camp as mutinies in the west (after General Nivelle's reckless sacrifice of French manpower at Chemin des Dames, April 1917), and revolution in the east, where in February a constitutional government had replaced the Tsarist regime and the new Premier Kerensky was engaged in the hopeless task of re-kindling stricken Russia's will to fight. Taking the short-term view, the Reich's war lords ignored the Reichstag resolution in favour of a compromise peace (introduced by the Centre leader Erzberger and supported by the Social Democrats and Left National Liberals in July 1917) and initiated an all-out drive for victory, which was to be attained in the early part of 1918, before America would have time to intervene decisively.

Preparatory to a great final offensive in the west, Ludendorff secured his eastern flank by permitting the exiled Russian Bolshevik leader, Lenin, to return from Switzerland via Germany and Sweden. Lenin took advantage of the democratic reforms introduced by Kerensky to appeal to the war-weary Russian masses with such good effect that another revolution in November 1917 brought the Bolsheviks to power and this new so-called Soviet government sued for peace within a month. Ludendorff's grand design thus seemed to be working out according to plan, even though some of the German units now being transferred westwards from the Russian front had been affected by Bolshevik anti-war propaganda. In fact anti-war feeling was by now spreading inside the Reich, where a break-away group of Left Socialists around Liebknecht (the only Reichstag deputy to vote against war credits in 1914), fomented strikes among munition workers and others. The strike-wave of January 1918 was suppressed without much difficulty, and in March the start of the last great offensive in the west was accompanied by the announcement of the Russo-German peace-terms at Brest-Litovsk. Since under this treaty the mineral and food resources of the Ukraine were added to those already under the control of the central powers, Germany seemed in those early months of 1918 to be almost within grasp of victory —but it was not to be. A neutral war-correspondent described Germany's military situation at that time as 'brilliant but hopeless'. Ludendorff was still pushing the Allies back in July, but although the Anglo-French line retreated, it did not break. In August the unified Allied Command under Marshal Foch commenced a counter-attack which, backed by growing numbers of freshly-arrived American troops, was inexorably gaining ground. At the same time the area under control of the central powers was shrinking rapidly as a result of British advances into Turkey's Arabic dependencies, and of Bulgaria's dropping out of the war in September 1918. Austria-Hungary, too, was in desperate straits, for at this stage its Slav subject peoples felt national independence to be within their grasp for the first time in centuries; did President Wilson's Fourteen Points (intended as the basis of an equitable peace settlement) not contain a key-clause about the 'self-determination of nations'?

The end was in sight for the Empire of the Habsburgs, and for the Reich of the Hohenzollerns. The much-vaunted Weltpolitik of their last occupant of the Imperial throne had not resulted in establishing German power across the oceans and the continents. Instead it had contributed to the coming of America into Europe and the coming of Communism to Russia, two events of incalculable future significance. And so before the onset of a fifth hunger-ridden war winter the Second Reich expired by the same process as had attended its birth forty-seven years earlier: the arbitrament of arms.

The First and Second Reichs

The history of Germany, more than that of most other countries, has been characterised by paradox and extremes.

Since the foundation of the First Reich, she was engaged in a civilising mission among her neighbours, especially in the east—yet the means she employed towards that end were not infrequently barbaric. Her medieval Emperors aspired to lead the whole of Christendom—and often lacked a following among their own subjects.

At the beginning of modern times she sounded the clarion call to religious freedom—and sank herself into ever-greater depths of political and economic servitude.

When Bismarck was born she was a European backwater renowned for Goethe's poetry and Beethoven's music—when he died she was a world power, her fame resting on Moltke's strategy and the molten steel of Krupp. Her people desired strength abroad—and evinced weakness in the face of authority at home.[1] Her Kaiser called himself pro-British—and remained wedded to the concepts of Weltpolitik and naval expansion. Her diplomats exerted a moderating influence on her alliance-partner Austria during the Balkan Wars (1912–13)—and during the crucial weeks after the Sarajevo shootings reverted to the attitude expressed in Chancellor von Bülow's dispatch to the Austrian Foreign Minister, Aerenthal, at the time of the Bosnian crisis (1908): 'I shall regard

---

[1] Cf. Carl Zuckmayer's comedy *The Captain of Köpenick*, in which a tramp hires a captain's uniform from an old clothes dealer, and in this disguise gets a local government official to hand him a large sum of money without having to produce any authorisation, the uniform sufficing.

the decision you ultimately come to as that dictated by circumstances'.

Going beyond these apparent contradictions, we must now look for some of the more permanent factors underlying her historical development, and since our introductory chapters conclude with the First World War, we are going to make militarism our starting-point. This does not imply that German militarism can be held responsible for the outbreak of the Great War. But its very existence was a factor contributing to that state of tension in international society which found its eventual discharge in the Armageddon of 1914–18.

German (i.e. Prussian) militarism was rooted in political as well as social history and in geography. Successive, and on the whole successful, wars with Poland, Sweden, Russia, Denmark, Austria and France, had marked every step of Prussia's progress from an electorate to a kingdom and eventually, to the nucleus of an Empire; the Second Reich's very baptism had been on the battle-fields of France.

The geographical factors tending to promote Prussia's (and subsequently Germany's) warlike tendencies were a total absence of clearly defined natural frontiers in the east, and a partial one in the west[1], as well as a position in the centre of the continental land-mass, which seemed to present Germany's enemies with a unique opportunity for keeping her in a state of encirclement. A preoccupation with soldiering to offset these handicaps was powerfully assisted by the prolongation of feudal modes of living well into the nineteenth century. The typical lord-and-subject relationships of a Junker estate approximated easily to that existing between officers and men on the barrack-square.

Throughout the whole of this period, the feudal officer caste had been considered—next to the princely dynasties—the highest stratum of society. The topmost army rank to which a middle-class person could aspire in peace time was that of officer of the reserve. (A celebrated pre-war cartoon showed Reich Chancellor Bethmann-Hollweg, a commoner by birth, wearing reserve officer's uniform and standing to attention on the steps leading up to the

[1] Where the Rhine, for part of its middle and lower course, flows through areas of German settlement on either bank.

Reichstag, while a posse of generals preceded him into the building.)

Heraclitus' dictum describing 'war as the father of all things', had long been a standard subject on which theses were written at German universities. The beneficial effect of war had been expounded to the educated classes by some of Germany's most eminent academics. The philosopher Hegel who had succeeded Fichte as professor at the University of Berlin, had written, 'Just as the blowing of the winds preserves the seas from the foulness resulting from prolonged calm, so is war between states an instrument for purifying the ethical health of nations corrupted by a long peace'.

The great historian Treitschke, had argued along similar lines: 'Peace is a state of sloth leaving the individual preoccupied with selfish concerns, whereas the grandeur of war consists in the utter annihilation of puny man in the great conception of the state'. Treitschke's state-worship was an application to secular ends of the Christian dictum, 'in Thy service is perfect freedom'. This concept linked up with Hegel's hypothesis that history had followed a pre-determined upward path to reach its culmination in the Prussian state; Hegel's conclusion had been that since man could only be truly free by moving with the trend of history, submission to the (Prussian) state ought to be the logical choice of every individual.

The deification of such morally neutral forces as History or the State indicated a growing enfeeblement of Christian belief. Whilst Germany of course shared this tendency with other countries affected by the Enlightenment of the eighteenth century, her uniquely deep-seated division into two rival churches had made matters worse.[1] Since Leibnitz's failure to provide the philosophical basis for reconciling the Catholic and Protestant faiths—in his book *La Théodicée*—no further attempts had been made in the direction of Christian reunion. The late nineteenth-century writer Lagarde had started a new trend of pseudo-religious thinking by rejecting all existing churches and demanding 'a national German religion corresponding to the nature of the German nation as willed by God'.

[1] German anti-religious feeling found its most powerful advocate in the late nineteenth-century philosopher Nietzsche.

As if in response to Lagarde's demands for a type of religion appropriate to a particular nation instead of mankind, Jesus Himself had been, if not Germanised, then at least, 'racially re-classified' as a fair-haired, blue-eyed Galilean, by Houston S. Chamberlain. This ex-Englishman and naturalised German had dedicated the whole of his massive *Foundations of the Nineteenth Century*, to the proposition that all progress throughout history had been achieved solely by the genius inherent in the Nordic (or Aryan) races, whose finest substance was represented by the German people: a substance which must never be sullied by contact with such inferior races as Jews or Negroes. (This emphasis on heredity and the breeding of good stock also owed a lot of its contemporary significance to the popularisation of Darwin's theories on human evolution and to a vogue of plays such as Ibsen's *Ghosts*, that treated of hereditary disease and similar problems.)

A specially significant aspect of Chamberlain's racism was its anti-Jewish emphasis. Pogroms of particular savagery had already stained the Rhineland towns at the time of the medieval Crusades and anti-semitic animus had, with varying degrees of virulence, coloured the opinions of such outstanding Germans as Martin Luther, the philosopher Fichte, and the composer Richard Wagner. (Wagner, whose very operas were an invocation of Germany's tribal past, described the role of the Jews in art as that of parasites incapable of creating anything of their own.)

After the 1873 stock exchange crash Treitschke's slogan 'The Jews are our misfortune' had gained wide currency. It was at about this time that anti-semitism was first formulated (by the journalist, W. Marr), to express the distinction between the old method of attacking the Jew on account of his religion (which he could, and not infrequently did, change), and the new, which attacked him on account of his inescapable race. Antisemitic movements, modelled on Schönerer's extremist Pan-German party in Austria, were inaugurated by the Court Chaplain Stöcker and other minor political figures. They made little lasting impact in the Reichstag, but the universities were amazingly prone to the racist virus. By the outbreak of war 30 per cent of the All-German League's membership were Ph.Ds, and most student fraternities debarred Jewish members who were furthermore forbidden to be challenged to duels since they were, by definition, devoid of honour.

These forms of social discrimination were irksome, but did not prevent some Jews from rising to the highest positions in the economy. A. Ballin built up Germany's most important shipping company, and E. Rathenau[1] shared honours with the non-Jew, W. von Siemens, in promoting the stupendous growth of the Reich's electrical industry (see p. 37). In all, the rate of industrial expansion had been most impressive under the Second Empire, whose government showed due concern for the interests of big business. And German business was big, since most industries were run by cartels—cartel agreements even being held to possess legal sanctions—in contrast to the anti-monopoly safeguards of contemporary British and American legislation.

The tendency for individual firms to merge into large units arose out of the speed and scope of industrialisation, the fear of a recurrence of the 1873 crash, and the drive towards eliminating internal competition connected with the abandonment of Free Trade. Although the trade unions were growing in importance throughout the period, the practice of collective bargaining, with its attendant effect of reducing profit-margins, only became generally accepted shortly before the war. Mention needs also to be made of the fact that German industry had quite an appreciable influence on the drive towards this war and on its conduct. Protectionism had meant that the Reich's manufacturers could compete with their free-trading British counterparts on unequal terms abroad, since profits from the guaranteed home market enabled them to underprice their rivals.

This so-called economic imperialism exacerbated the pre-war relationship among the great powers no less than did the activities of the All-German, Colonial and Navy Leagues, all of which had links with industry and numbered 'Ruhr barons' of the calibre of Krupp, Kierdorff or Stinnes among their sponsors. Even the war aims of the High Command were to some extent coloured by the expansionist requirements of heavy industry. Thus it was not purely from considerations of prestige or even of strategic advantage, that the Reich government, right up to the last offensive of

---

[1] His son, Walter Rathenau, became successively controller of the wartime economy and peace-time Foreign Minister.

the war, could envisage no other post-war frontiers for Germany than those which included the mineral wealth of the Liège-Longwy-Brie region.

The paradox of Ludendorff and Hindenburg launching huge battles in pursuit of these objectives a full year after the majority of the elected representatives of the German people had gone on record in favour of a compromise peace (Reichstag Peace Resolution of July 1917), is, however, to be explained less in terms of the machinations of big business than of the weakness of German democracy under the Bismarckian system itself. The existence of an opposition majority on an issue which would elsewhere have toppled the government produced hardly any repercussions inside the Reich. To attribute this impotence of Parliament primarily to a war-time aversion to changing horses in mid-stream, or even to the effectiveness of the constitutional arrangement vesting control over the government in the Emperor, is to leave one important element out of account—the opposition's lack of purpose. The possibility of a majority anti-government coalition of Left National Liberals, Centre and Social Democrats inside the Reichstag had actually existed ever since the last peace-time elections, of 1912, when the Socialists had emerged as the strongest party in the country. Yet an opposition bloc of this type did not come about; the parties had for too long been accustomed to playing the political game according to Bismarck's rules for it to occur to them that they might be able to change those rules.

The weakness of German parliamentarianism dated back to the failure of the Prussian majority opposition to the Army Reforms (1862) and beyond that to the glaring fiasco of the Frankfurt Assembly in 1848-9. The corollary to the adage 'nothing succeeds like success' is that likewise nothing fails like failure. Lacking the self-confidence which could stem only from having helped to shape the course of events, the parties fitted easily into Bismarck's system, which excluded them from participation in government. In this way they degenerated into little more than pressure groups or lobbies on behalf of the respective social or religious group that voted for them. To the functionaries ensconced in the various party machines the government did not appear as a commanding height to be captured, or even successfully assaulted; rather did it resemble a towering rock face from which assiduous chipping, in the form of Reichstag pressure, might prise loose valuable flints, i.e. concessions for the interest group they happened to represent. Now that under the impact of imminent defeat large cracks were appearing in this rock, a true turning-point in the history of Germany had been reached. Its after-effects are the subject matter of our subsequent chapters.

3

From World War to Civil War

THE GREAT WAR ended on 11 November 1918, with the German acceptance of the Allied surrender terms. On the 10th, Kaiser Wilhelm II had crossed the frontier into Holland (and permanent exile) shortly after the formation of a new government under the right-wing Socialist, Ebert, an ex-saddler. This government ✗ proclaimed Germany a republic amid a welter of demonstrations, strikes and mutinies in units of the navy and army.

The Army High Command which had controlled German affairs since August 1914, was still the motive force behind events right up to the end of the war. General Ludendorff had realised by September 1918 that the war could not be won under any circumstances, and that drastic changes were required immediately to shield Germany from having to face the full consequences of defeat. He had accordingly instructed the Chancellor, Prince Max of Baden, to take Social Democrat ministers into the government and to open secret armistice negotiations with the American President, Woodrow Wilson. The presence of Socialists in the government would help in smoothing over the difficulties involved in making contacts with enemies whom Germany had opposed in a murderous struggle for over four years. This was due to the fact that during previous Reichstag debates on Germany's war aims, the Social Democrats had insisted that the peace-settlement should involve no annexations of non-German territory; their record on this issue would make them more acceptable to the Allies than any other German political group.

In order to improve Germany's bargaining position at future

peace talks, Ludendorff wanted the armistice to come into force before Allied forces had actually set foot on German soil. This, plus the growing pressure of anti-war and left-wing sentiment in the armed forces and industrial centres, led to the Chancellor, Max of Baden's, replacement by Friedrich Ebert. In the hour of military collapse the reins of government passed from a prince to a former saddle-maker. Germany in travail gave birth to a Republican form of government, and from the very out-set the new republic was disfigured by the ugly birthmark of defeat.

Ebert's caretaker administration maintained uneasy control during the first post-war winter when, on account of the continua-tion of the Allied blockade, cold and hunger were widespread, especially in the towns. An important factor contributing to Ebert's success during those difficult months was the support given to the government by the military. For although demobilisa-tion proceeded with all possible speed, certain dependable regiments were being kept on an active footing. These were assigned police duties; more important still, the General Staff was not disbanded.

The new republic's first general election (in January 1919), confirmed Ebert in office. It also chose the delegates to the National Assembly whose duty it would be to work out a con-stitution for the new state. Because Berlin happened to be the scene of political disturbances, this assembly met at Weimar, a sleepy provincial town, which because of past associations with the poets Goethe and Schiller holds the same place in the country's affection as does Stratford-on-Avon in England.

The Berlin riots had been sparked off by the Spartakists, revolutionary socialists who aimed at the overthrow of Ebert's government. They charged Ebert with betraying the cause of socialism by collaborating with reactionary army chiefs and refusing to nationalise heavy industry. The famous Spartakist leaders, Karl Liebknecht and Rosa Luxemberg, were captured by right-wing irregular forces (*Freikorps*) acting in concert with the Social Democrat Minister of the Interior, Noske, and sum-marily shot. The rising collapsed, but some of the surviving Spartakists subsequently formed the nucleus of the German Communist Party.

June 1919 saw similar events enacted in Munich, the Bavarian capital, where a self-styled 'Soviet' government had temporarily taken over. Munich was 'liberated' by a combined force of regular soldiers, Freikorps and peasants' rifle clubs. The 'Soviet' leaders, pacifist poets and muddle-headed idealist reformers with hardly one genuine Bolshevik among them, were captured and shot. The spectre of Red Revolution seemed banished, at least for the time being.

Shortly afterwards, the attention of the whole of Germany was diverted away from the disturbed internal scene, to the Palace of Versailles, where her representatives had been asked to sign the peace treaty which was to serve as the basis of the country's relations with the victorious Allies. Germany had no say in negotiating the Versailles Treaty which had been formulated after months of wrangling between the leaders of the chief Allied powers, Wilson of the United States, Lloyd George of Great Britain and Clemenceau of France.

When the treaty terms were published in Germany there was an outcry. Large sections of the public, especially supporters of the right-wing parties, denounced acceptance of the treaty as an act of treason against the Fatherland. The Social Democrat leader Scheidemann resigned from the government, exclaiming dramatically: 'May the hand wither that signs this Treaty'. In certain circles a renewal of the war was canvassed as the only honourable alternative to acceptance. General Groener, Ludendorff's successor, however, warned President Ebert that such action would lack every prospect of success in view of the vast military superiority of the Allies, and that the treaty would have to be signed. Even Foreign Minister Brockdorff-Rantzau, who led the German delegation at Versailles, opposed acceptance, but he professed to see advantages accruing to Germany from the actual circumstances of the signing: 'By not insisting on dictating terms to us in Berlin and by inviting us to Versailles instead, the Allies have given the government a chance of playing down the extent of the defeat to the Germans at home. . . . We shall win the final battle.' The Versailles Treaty, signed on 28 June 1919,[1] contained the following main terms:

[1] On that day many German newspapers appeared with a black band of mourning across their front page.

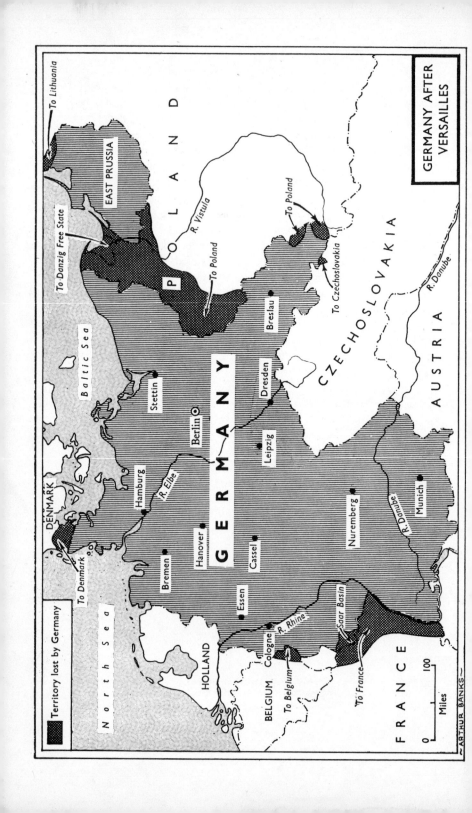

GERMANY AFTER VERSAILLES

Territory lost by Germany

To Lithuania

EAST PRUSSIA

To Danzig Free State

Baltic Sea

POLAND

To Poland

To Poland

R. Vistula

To Poland

Breslau

To Czechoslovakia

CZECHOSLOVAKIA

R. Danube

AUSTRIA

Stettin

Dresden

Berlin

GERMANY

Leipzig

Hamburg

R. Elbe

Hanover

Munich

R. Danube

Nuremberg

Bremen

Cassel

Denmark

To Denmark

North Sea

Essen

Cologne

R. Rhine

Saar Basin

HOLLAND

BELGIUM

To Belgium

To France

FRANCE

0   100
Miles

ARTHUR BANKS

Germany was to surrender her colonial empire and her fleet.
Her army was to be limited to 100,000 men and restricted in
its range of weapons.

A zone along the right bank of the Rhine was to be de-mili-
tarised; the left bank placed under Allied occupation for
fifteen years.

France and Belgium were to be paid a huge but undefined
German indemnity to compensate them for ravages suffered
during the war.

Germany was to cede Alsace-Lorraine back to France,
Eupen-Malmédy to Belgium, North Schleswig to Denmark,
West Prussia and parts of Silesia to Poland. (This meant that
East Prussia would be cut off by the Polish Corridor.)

Danzig and the Saar were to be severed from the Reich; the
former as an autonomous Free City and the latter under the
League of Nations (the Wilson-inspired forerunner of UNO).

Germans suspected of war crimes were to be put on trial, etc.

To most Germans these terms appeared not merely vindictive,
but unjust in the extreme, a travesty of the peace without annexations assurances held out by Wilson in his Fourteen Points, and an
attempt to saddle Germany with the consequences of a war-guilt
which they did not accept. Even the counsels of the Allies had been
divided, with the Anglo-Saxon powers exasperated by France's
overriding preoccupation with 'security', i.e. protection against a
German threat which had now been removed for a long time to
come. Some British and American officials even held it to be a bad
augury for the peace of the world that a war prosecuted to prevent
one power dominating a whole continent should terminate with
another power (i.e. France) in that very position.

The Germans in 1919 and subsequently, did not tire of inveigh-
ing against the iniquity of Versailles; they showed a total disregard
for what their own leaders had done fifteen months earlier, when
Russia had sued for peace after the Bolshevik Revolution (March
1918). At Brest-Litovsk the representative of the German High
Command, General Hoffmann, had dictated terms[1] depriving
Russia of a quarter of its area, two-fifths of its population, three-
quarters of its coal and iron, and four-fifths of its beet sugar. This

[1] Which Lenin's emissary Trotsky accepted in the hope that a proletarian
revolution inside Germany would speedily bring about their abrogation.

treaty had been approved by the whole Reichstag with the exception of the Socialists.

The bitter controversies raging around the Versailles Treaty and its acceptance by the Ebert government had in the meantime obscured the constitutional labours of the Weimar National Assembly which had gone on from February until August 1919. This new Constitution, under which Germany was to be governed until Hitler's accession in 1933, stated: 'In the German Republic all power emanates from the people'. This was far and away its most important single innovation, since it gave Germany responsible government for the first time in history. In detail there were certain similarities with Bismarck's arrangements, e.g. the various provinces or Länder (such as Prussia, Bavaria and Saxony, etc.) kept their separate control over education, health, justice, and the like. The central government in Berlin dealt with foreign affairs, defence, finance and economics, etc. The head of state was the President, who was directly elected by all the voters, and who was given wide emergency powers; he could rule by decree if the Reichstag lacked a stable majority for carrying on the country's government. Important clauses of the constitution guaranteed all citizens equality before the law, freedom from arbitrary arrest, and freedom of speech, association and conscience.

The Reichstag with a membership of 580 was the supreme law-making body. It was elected by all citizens over twenty, in direct secret ballot by proportional representation. Proportional representation meant that if a party, for instance, secured 5 per cent of the votes cast during a general election, it would receive exactly that proportion of all parliamentary seats (i.e. 29 out of 580). Compared to the British system this was much fairer to the smaller parties, but it had the unfortunate result of making it impossible for any single party to secure a majority over all the others in the Reichstag. Consequently coalition governments had to be formed from among such of the larger parties as were capable of sinking their differences sufficiently to work together. This means that the tenure of office of successive cabinets tended to be brief and that a lot of political horse-trading usually went on behind the scenes before a new government could be formed.

In spite of these blemishes, the Weimar Constitution, with its systems of checks and balances—President as against Parliament,

Centre as against the Provinces—still seemed as good a mechanism as could be devised by the skill of lawyers and politicians for conducting the all-important business of government on the basis of freedom under the law. But those who had framed the constitution had failed to take into account the first pre-condition of its workability: an electorate that wanted to be governed on the basis of freedom under the law. From the very beginning democracy in the Weimar Republic laboured under an enormous handicap: it had been introduced in the hour of defeat, not by the will of the German people, but in order to fill the vacuum left by the collapse of the Kaiser's government with an arrangement acceptable to the victorious Allies.

As a consequence the middle-of-the-road parties, on whose backing constitutional government depended, were hemmed in on either side by extremists of the Left and the Right.[1] Those anti-democratic groups had a mass-following which varied in inverse proportion to the German republic's prosperity and stability, but whose numbers only sank below danger level for the Weimar state during the years 1924–28.

If the main challenge in 1919 had come from the Left, the following year brought an extreme right-wing attempt at capturing the government. Freikorps veterans of frontier skirmishes against Poles and Bolsheviks occupied Berlin and proclaimed a new regime, headed by Dr Kapp. Kapp's programme was the suppression of democracy and the trade unions at home, and resistance to the Versailles Treaty abroad. He had counted on the support of the army and the bureaucracy—but the military were split and the civil service remained loyal to Ebert. A strike of Berlin's workers quickly put an end to the Kapp *putsch* (armed seizure of power).

By the end of 1920, it therefore appeared as if the Weimar Republic, having survived attempts on its life from the Left and the Right, was at last settling down to a period of greater stability. Yet beneath the surface tensions continued to build up, erupting every so often with sudden violence. In 1921 Germany was startled to hear that the Catholic Centre leader, Erzberger, had been

[1] The middle-of-the-road parties were the Social Democrats, the Catholic Centre, the Democrats (the pre-war Left National Liberals) and the People's Party (formerly National Liberals). The extreme Left consisted of the Communists and Socialist splinter groups; the extreme Right of the Nationalist and Nazi parties.

57

THE GREAT INFLATION

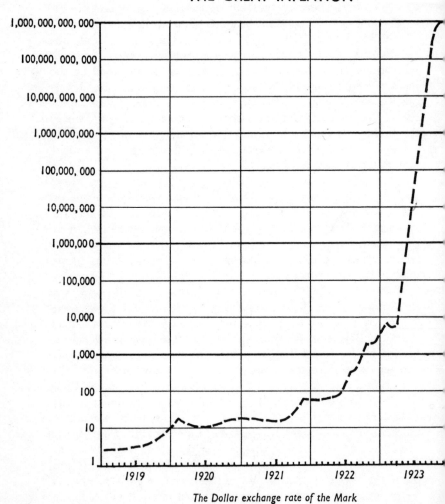

The Dollar exchange rate of the Mark

assassinated. Erzberger had been one of Germany's representatives at Versailles and had put his signature to the 'treaty of shame'. In the eyes of the extreme Nationalists, that had been an act of high treason. During periods of lawlessness in the Middle Ages, public-spirited Germans had formed private courts, so-called *Fehme* tribunals, to try evil-doers in their absence and pass sentence on them. The Fehme had then appointed executioners to carry out those sentences. This practice had been revived by extreme right-wing groups in the German Republic to deal with 'enemies of the Fatherland'. Erzberger was their first prominent quarry.

The next famous Fehme victim was Foreign Minister Walter Rathenau, a Democrat, who on the vexed issue of Germany's reparation obligations to the Allies, had unequivocally stated: 'It is in keeping with the dignity of a debtor to pay'. In Rathenau's opinion Germany could only work her passage back into the confidence of the western powers by a policy of fulfilment. This, plus the fact that he was Jewish, had drawn the wrath of the extreme Right down upon his head, and the murderous jingle 'Bump off the Yid Rathenau, the goddam Jewish sow', chanted in beer-gardens and daubed on hoardings, had created an atmosphere in which his assassination was almost a foregone conclusion. Two of his murderers died resisting arrest; the other Fehme-conspirators were brought to trial. The main accused received a 15-year sentence, of which he only served seven, and was subsequently pardoned, and a heavily implicated accomplice, Ernst von Salomon, spent five years in prison, during which time he wrote a best-seller about the circumstances surrounding the murder.

Most other Fehme assassins showed greater skill in evading the police. Those who were caught and charged in the courts had relatively little to fear. The judges, patriotic government officials who in the main had been put on the bench in the days of the Kaiser, inclined to leniency in dealing with dedicated young men of obvious, if misguided, patriotism.

During the period 1918–22 no fewer than 376 political murders took place in Germany. Of those 22 were committed by the Left, and 354 by the Right. Convictions by the courts totalled 62, including ten death sentences. In each instance the capital punishment applied to cases of left-wing violence; none of the 354 murders perpetrated by the Right led to anything other than terms of imprisonment.

This political instability was made worse by the drain on Germany's resources arising from the Allied demands for reparations. An over-all figure of £6,600,000,000 had been decided on in 1921, to be paid off in annual instalments. This undermined the stability of the currency; the mark dropped in value throughout 1922 and reparation payments could not be maintained. Early in 1923 Germany was in default.

The French government, led by Poincaré, believed that the Germans were trying to cheat their way out of meeting their obligations. They decided to enforce payment by sending French troops into the Ruhr, the hub of Germany's heavy industry, to remain in occupation until the defaulters had honoured their commitments.

The occupation of the Ruhr by powerful French units lasted eight months. It was a period throughout which an undeclared state of war existed between the occupying forces and the German population. Miners and steel workers refused to continue working. Although the government provided them with strike pay, they suffered considerable hardship at a time when money was losing its value more and more. Nationalistic anti-French clamour rose to a new pitch throughout the country; chauvinist agitators were elated to see public opinion veering more and more to the Right, especially in the province of Bavaria. The Ruhr occupation, partly carried out by French military units drawn from the African colonies, presented them with an image reflecting the depth of Germany's degradation under a weak government: armed negroes swaggering through Ruhr towns, affronting the honour of German women!

Finally, in September 1923, the French agreed to withdraw their forces on the understanding that the new German government led by Stresemann, of the People's Party, would punctually fulfil its reparation commitments. Both sides could claim a victory, but there was one undisputed loser, the German currency, still further devalued as the result of the paralysis of the Ruhr industry. In 1914 the exchange rate of £1 sterling had been 15 marks, in 1922, 760 marks, in January 1923, 72,000 marks, and by November of that year, 16,000,000,000 marks. By this time, the Reichsbank

had 300 paper mills and 2,000 printing establishments working on
24-hour shifts to provide it with the paper currency that was
flooding Germany, and wiping out the value of all savings. This
financial collapse was almost paralleled in the political sphere.
For a time during the autumn of 1923, it seemed as if the Republic
would dissolve in a welter of extremist insurrections. This danger
was eventually overcome, but at the time it looked very formidable
indeed.

Of those risings the one with the most ominous significance for
the future occurred in Bavaria, on the instigation of a local
politician by the name of Adolf Hitler. He had started his Nazi
party in Munich four years earlier, and since then the number of
his supporters had steadily grown. In 1922 another leader of an
extreme right-wing movement had seized power in Italy under
conditions of similar internal instability. Mussolini's example
influenced Hitler in many ways, from the type of salute he adopted
for the Party to his attempt to carry out a march on Berlin,
modelled on Mussolini's march on Rome which had led to the
overthrow of Italian democracy.

In order to stage his march on Berlin, Hitler needed a secure
base. According to his calculations, Bavaria could be turned into
such a base. This large Catholic province had been an independent
state under its own royal house of Wittelsbach for centuries before
Bismarck's unification of 1871. Even after its fusion with the rest
of Germany, Bavarian particularism had been respected, with a
Wittelsbach remaining on the throne in Munich until Germany
became a republic in 1918. A separate Bavarian army and civil
service were similarly still in existence. Some of these institutions
continued under the Republic, whose advent, as far as many
Bavarians were concerned, had been marred by the terrifying
episode of the Munich Soviet. Since that outcrop of Communism
on their own soil most Bavarians had been politically further to the
Right than the rest of their fellow countrymen.

When Ebert and Stresemann called off the passive resistance
campaign in the Ruhr and agreed to the resumption of reparation
payments, the cry of treason rang shrilly through Germany, echoed
more loudly in Bavaria than elsewhere.

Shortly afterwards, taking advantage of the economic distress
caused by the run-away inflation, local Communists seized power

in the provinces of Thuringia and Saxony. These uprisings were short-lived and easily brought under control by the forces of the central government. But they added grist to the mills of Nazi propaganda. Warning cries of 'Red Peril' underscored their strident demands that Germany be purged of a government which allowed the Fatherland to be trodden underfoot by the French in the west and the Bolsheviks in the east.

To rid Germany of this government, Hitler placed his Nazi storm-troopers on a civil-war footing. The first objective was to be the capture of power in Bavaria, to be followed by the march on Berlin and control of the whole country. The Bavarian Land government realised the gravity of this threat to public order, and its members, conservative-minded Catholics, decided to grant emergency powers to a specially appointed State Commissioner, von Kahr, that he might take such steps as were required to avert Hitler's insurrection.

Von Kahr's attachment to the cause of the German Republic, however, was not particularly strong; as a fervent Bavarian monarchist he had not forgiven those who had driven the Wittelbachs off the throne.

But the Bavarian government was not the only German authority which at this juncture had to turn to men whose attitude to the Republic was at least doubtful. Alarmed by the fact that the central government's writ was virtually ceasing to run in large areas of the country, Chancellor Stresemann invoked the emergency regulations of the Weimar Constitution and granted special powers to the army chief, General von Seeckt. Von Seeckt, whose overriding aim was the revival of Germany's military might, felt that for the time being this purpose would be served best by support for the lawful authorities, and therefore loyally assisted the Republic.

Less than five years had elapsed since the monarchist, anti-democratic High Command had in the hour of defeat acted as godfather to the infant Republic—now it was once again the guardian of Germany's political destiny.

The Bavarian Army District was commanded by General von Lossow who, like State Commissioner von Kahr, was at heart a Bavarian monarchist, desiring above all else a restoration of the Wittelbachs to the throne at Munich. Like State Commissioner

von Kahr, but unlike his immediate superior, von Seeckt, Lossow
saw in the gradual weakening of the central government's authority over the rest of the country a welcome opportunity for
Bavaria to break away and form an independent monarchy once
again.

These schemes for restoring the Wittelsbach monarchy cut
right across Hitler's political plans. He wanted to take over Bavaria
as a mere stepping-stone on the road to Berlin, and control over
the whole of Germany. Once the capital was in his grasp he intended to liquidate the governing 'gang of November criminals'
(i.e. the statesmen who had set up the new Republic in November
1918), and to make himself head of a government of the 'National
Revolution'.

On the evening of 8 November 1923, the Buergerbräu Keller,
a large beer hall on the outskirts of Munich, was the venue of a
crowded public meeting. Von Kahr, von Lossow and most other
Bavarian leaders were present. Hitler thought that the purpose of
the meeting was the proclamation of Bavaria's independence and
decided on immediate action. Whilst State Commissioner von
Kahr was speaking, armed Nazi storm-troopers surrounded the
building and covered every exit. Hitler entered the crowded hall
and strode towards the platform, firing two warning shots at the
ceiling. Into the stunned silence he hurled this dramatic announcement:

'The National Revolution has begun. The Bavarian and the
Reich's government are deposed. Storm-troops have occupied the
barracks of the army and police. A new government of National
Revolution is being formed. . . .'

Then, leaving the meeting to be further harangued by his chief
lieutenant Hermann Goering, a much decorated ex-fighter pilot,
Hitler withdrew into an adjacent room for urgent consultations
with von Kahr and von Lossow. He pressed them to identify the
Bavarian government and army with the 'National Revolution'.
They were reluctant to commit themselves to a course of action
fraught with unforeseeable dangers, but Hitler dramatically
flourished his revolver again and swore to kill both them and himself if they could not come to an agreement. Kahr and Lossow
were still hesitating, but just then ex-Field Marshal Ludendorff
arrived in answer to a previous summons, and with support from

the famous soldier, Hitler finally managed to convince the two waverers of the worthiness of his cause.

They jointly returned to the meeting hall and Hitler announced that the National Revolution had gained the support of the two most powerful men in Bavaria. The rally closed with the whole assembled company fervently intoning 'Deutschland, Deutschland über Alles' (Germany, Germany above all else), the national anthem of the Reich.

There followed a night of feverish Nazi preparation for the occupation of Munich, a large city of just under a million inhabitants.

SA[1] Chief of Staff Roehm, an ex-army captain, directed his storm-troopers in the setting up of machine-gun emplacements and barbed-wire entanglements at such strategic points as the building of the Bavarian Defence Ministry. The Buergerbräu tavern was turned into an armed camp, with swastika-armletted irregulars bivouacking in its cellars and grounds.

But the central authorities had not been caught unawares by these developments. When Commissioner von Kahr and General von Lossow returned to their respective headquarters, they received urgent orders from Berlin to take all measures necessary for preventing the Nazi putsch. In addition the aged Rupert of Wittelsbach, claimant to the throne of Bavaria, sent a personal appeal to the strongly monarchist Bavarian Officer Corps, adjuring them to honour their oath of allegiance to the lawful government.

Confronted with mounting evidence of official counter-measures, Hitler decided on a display of force for next morning. He planned a march of his supporters through the centre of Munich, calculating that this would meet with such popular response that the undecided von Kahr and von Lossow would no longer hesitate about which side to support.

A long column of rifle-carrying brownshirts set out in formation towards the city centre, cheered by great crowds lining the route. At its head strode Hitler; in the front rank beside him were ex-Field Marshal Ludendorff, Goering, Streicher and other Nazi leaders. Their progress was unopposed until they reached the large square in front of the Feldherrnhalle in the centre of Munich. At that point armed police barred the way and called upon the

[1] SA was the abbreviation used for the *Sturm Abteilungen* (storm-troopers).

marchers to stop. When the Nazis ignored this order, a volley of shots suddenly rang out, immediately followed by a wild scurry for cover.

Sixteen prostrate bodies remained on the ground while the rest abandoned the 'March on Berlin'—some, like Hitler, were taken into police custody and others, such as Goering, escaped abroad. The names of the sixteen dead were the first to be inscribed on the subsequent Nazi roll of honour.

Hitler's plans had ended in fiasco for the time being. The Nazi party was prohibited and he and Ludendorff had to face charges of high treason against the Republic. The case for the prosecution rested on the testimony of witnesses like von Kahr and von Lossow, who concealed as much of the truth as they could in order to salvage their tarnished reputations. The presiding judge, echoing his colleagues' words at the earlier 'Fehme trials', made much of the war record and 'unquestioned patriotism' of the men in the dock. Ludendorff was acquitted and Hitler, who had used every opportunity provided by the trial to turn the court room into a meeting hall from which his speeches reached the readers of all German papers, was given five years, this being the minimum term applicable in cases of treason.

He was conveyed to Landsberg jail where comfortable quarters, regular meals and frequent visits from well-wishers softened the rigours of prison life. Fellow inmates included Hitler's faithful assistant Rudolf Hess; together these two spent many fruitful hours in the prison library working out the first draft of what was later to become the Nazi 'Bible', the partly autobiographical, partly propagandist *Mein Kampf*.

4

Mein Kampf *and the Crash*

ADOLF HITLER had been born on 20 April 1889, at Braunau on the Inn, the river forming the boundary between Austria and Germany. His father, an Austrian customs official, had been resident in a succession of frontier towns. By the time Adolf was of school age Alois Hitler had retired from the customs administration and the family were living in an Upper Austrian village. Among the village children in his class, Adolf stood out by virtue of superior intelligence and at the age of ten, his family having in the meanwhile moved to the provincial capital Linz, he entered grammar school (the *Realschule*). He made indifferent progress and got very low marks in mathematics and German; at the end of the fourth year he was only allowed to pass up on condition of transferring elsewhere. On leaving school he airily announced his intention of commencing a course of private studies, but for the next two years he did little but draw, paint and visit the local opera house. He was also an avid reader, especially of the Redskin sagas of Karl May, an author at that time very popular with the German reading public.

Alois Hitler had died when Adolf was still at school. At the age of 18 Adolf received part of his paternal inheritance and moved to Vienna with the intention of studying at the Academy of Fine Arts. He did not manage to pass the entrance examination and stayed on in the capital in order to sit the examination again. Whilst proceeding with his private studies in drawing and architecture, he also started taking an interest in other topics such as politics and history.

Both the period and the place were opportune for a study of those two subjects. Vienna was the capital of the historic

Austro-Hungarian Empire, a major power in pre-war Europe, with a population of over 50,000,000, and an area stretching from the upper Rhine to the Lower Danube, and from the plains of Poland to the mountains of Montenegro. The aged Emperor Franz Joseph's subjects belonged to a dozen different races and spoke as many languages. The politics of the Empire were mainly carried on in terms of the conflict between its major racial groups: the dominant Austrians and Hungarians on one side and the various Slav nations such as the Czechs, Slovenes and Croats on the other. The Slavs resented their status as second-class citizens and were encouraged by Austria's enemies, Russia and Serbia, in claiming civic rights.

This growth of Slav national consciousness had provoked a strong reaction inside the Austrian Empire. The Pan-German movement, wanting at all costs to preserve German supremacy over inferior subject races, aimed at a union between Austria and the Reich and thereby offended the Emperor. At a lower level they tried everything in their power to block such Slav advances as the setting up of more Czech-speaking schools.

The Pan-Germans also attacked Catholicism, Socialism and the Jews: they opposed the Roman Church as international and therefore anti-German, Socialism because it split the Germans into opposing classes. The Jews came under heavy attack as a racially foreign body among Germans, besides which they were denounced as usurers, speculators, pacifists and agitators. The famous historian Treitschke's saying 'the Jews are our misfortune' became a Pan-German stock phrase.

The Catholic Church, secure in the support of the Imperial court, the middle classes and the peasantry, managed to withstand the attacks of the Pan-Germans. Its own political party, the Social Christians, were strongly entrenched both in the Austrian countryside and the capital, Vienna. Its leading personality, Dr Lueger, re-elected Mayor of Vienna for three consecutive terms, was an accomplished demagogue who, whilst himself under fire from the Pan-Germans, adroitly borrowed one of the most effective weapons from his opponents' armoury: antisemitism. Lueger proved that he was not to be outdone by the Pan-Germans when it came to Jew-baiting.

The youthful Hitler had been so impressed by him that he afterwards wrote, 'Dr Lueger had the rare gift of insight into human nature and never made the mistake of taking men to be better than they really were'.

This estimate of Lueger's qualities shows that the adolescent Hitler already had an instinctive grasp of the essentials of demagogic politics: an appreciation of the importance of mass psychology, coupled with total contempt for the masses. In Vienna the most important features of Hitler's world-picture were being filled in as a result of his contact with Lueger's demagoguery and Jew-baiting and the Pan-Germans' pathological hatred of Slavs and denunciation of Socialists. Their brand of hate-filled politics and the bombastic music of Wagner's Germanic operas were the vicarious excitements on which Hitler's mind fed during his lonely and frustrated stay in the Austrian capital.

He again failed to gain admission to the Academy of Art, but decided to remain in Vienna although he had by now almost exhausted his parental inheritance. Poverty compelled him to move into ever cheaper accommodation and frequently reduced him to seeking shelter among the human flotsam of the doss-houses. Still he managed to keep body and soul together somehow by hawking hand-painted postcards round seedy cafés.

In *Mein Kampf* he was later to refer to this period as the unhappiest of his entire life; not, however, on account of the squalor in which he was living, but because the Austrian capital filled him with loathing: 'Vienna with its promiscuous swarm of foreign races, Czechs, Poles, Croats and the like, all of them battening on that old nursery of German culture—and in addition the Jews—germ-carriers infecting the whole of society, to be found here, there and everywhere.'

In 1913 Hitler suddenly exchanged Vienna for Munich as his place of residence. The Austrian authorities had been sending him call-up notices for some time, but by frequently changing his address he had contrived to evade them. When it appeared that officialdom was about to catch up with him, he hurriedly moved to Bavaria. There he continued his previous mode of existence, although inwardly he was far happier now, because Munich, as he wrote later, was 'a city purely German in population and architecture, and furthermore immune to the alien canker eating into the heart of the Austrian Empire.'

The outbreak of the Great War in the summer of 1914 led to

patriotic outbursts all over the Reich. A still extant photograph taken in the main square of Munich shows Hitler as part of a vast cheering crowd, his face visibly expressing the emotion gripping everyone in those hectic August days. He volunteered for service in a Bavarian regiment, rose to corporal's rank, was wounded, and subsequently awarded the Iron Cross, first class. (There is some controversy on the last point; one theory has it that Hitler received this important military decoration through the good offices of his friend, General Ludendorff, after the war.) Whatever the facts of the case, there can be no doubt that in contrast to the frustrations of peace-time, Hitler experienced true fulfilment in the front line. This lone wolf lacking in all social graces, to whom conversation meant talking at people instead of to them, was always impatient to get back to the trenches, alike after short spells of home leave or a prolonged stay at a base hospital.

The news of Germany's defeat struck him a tremendous blow. The temporary blindness afflicting him in the autumn of 1918, which he attributed to an Allied gas attack, may in fact have been a hysterical reaction to the shock of discovering that the war had been lost. Upon discharge from a military sanatorium he returned to his unit which in 1919 was stationed at Munich. Selected for a political training course in which reliable NCOs were taught by their officers how best to combat left-wing ideas in the army and among the civilian population, he was assigned the task of reporting on the activities of a newly-formed party.

The National Socialist German Workers' party was one of a host of political groups springing up in Bavaria during the disturbed aftermath of the war. It was little more than a discussion circle frequented by self-important reformers with crankish ideas on how to put the country to rights. Shortly after being accepted as a member, Hitler ousted the original leadership and started trans- — see p.61. forming an obscure body of armchair politicians into a force to be reckoned with in Bavarian public life. This was shown early in 1920 when an audience of 2,000 gathered to hear him read out the programme he had drafted for the National Socialist Workers' party. It consisted of 25 points, many of which had been drawn from the common pool of all contemporary German nationalist thinking (e.g. demands for abrogating the Treaty of Versailles, for the union of Austria with Germany and for the withdrawal of citizenship rights from Jews). But there were certain additional items in the programme which showed a left-wing inspiration compatible with the Socialist label the party had tacked on to its name: the nationalisation of all department stores, the banning of speculation in land and the abolition of unearned incomes.

This peculiar combination of nationalist and socialist catch phrases was one of the Nazi party's greatest assets. Whereas other extremist groups were either dedicated to the cause of the Fatherland, if they were of the Right, or to that of the workers, if they were of the Left, the National Socialists laid claim to being equally concerned with both. Hitler could thus be all things to all men. In this lay his great advantage over all rival nationalist leaders, who as ex-officers or industrialists held little attraction for a working-class following. The Communists, on the other hand, were incapable of extending the source of their support beyond the minority of 'militant' workers. Being committed to the class struggle and to Soviet Russia they could not effectively exploit the nationalist discontent defeat had engendered throughout Germany.

An opportunistically hybrid ideology was only one of Hitler's political trumps; among the others his gift for public speaking was undoubtedly the greatest. Lenin once said that an idea becomes a force when it captures the masses. That was precisely what Hitler set out to do, at first by no other means than his vocal chords. From street corner oratory he swiftly progressed to the haranguing of large crowds in meeting halls, but irrespective of the venue he almost invariably managed to lash both himself and his audience into a state of frenzy.

These rabble-rousing scenes took place in a setting of uniforms, banners and flags. They were introduced by marching songs, and after every climax of eloquence, cheer-leaders got the audience to respond with the rhythmic chanting of Nazi slogans. Another feature quite typical of these meetings was the deliberate use of violence. For this purpose, Hitler had created a special section of the Nazi party, the storm-troopers (or SA), whose task it was to attack hecklers with truncheons and knuckle-dusters. When not 'stewarding' at their own meetings the storm-troopers were employed in breaking up those of their opponents.

The brutality of the storm-troopers, far from being played down by Party propagandists, was openly avowed. Hitler interpreted it as visible proof of the brownshirts' fervent attachment to the cause. The mixture of mob-oratory and violence paid dividends within a short while. The Party built up a mass-following in Munich, 'the cradle of the movement', and Hitler was afforded entry into polite Bavarian society. By 1922 the man who a decade earlier had bedded down with tramps in the doss-houses of Vienna, was attending receptions at the house of the piano-manufacturer Bechstein and paying visits to Richard Wagner's family at Bayreuth. In that mecca of German opera lovers he was cordially received by the great composer's daughter and her husband, the aged Houston Chamberlain. Chamberlain's pre-war writings on the superiority of the Nordic race had suggested to many Germans that they were destined to rule the world. On his Bayreuth pilgrimage, Hitler could therefore pay homage to two sources of his own inspiration, the romanticism of music and of race.

But to the rising party-leader the value of these new contacts was more than merely sentimental. His newly-found supporters soon contributed sufficiently large funds to enable the Party to bring out its own daily paper, the *Völkische Beobachter*. The propagandist effectiveness of the National Socialists was further boosted when Julius Streicher, a Nuremberg primary school teacher, joined them. Streicher was editor of a poisonous weekly called *Der Stuermer*, whose every issue harped on the Jews to the exclusion of any other topic. In this it was ultimately so successful that a major share in preparing the minds of the German public for the murder of 6,000,000 human beings can be attributed to it.

Another important recruit at this stage was Alfred Rosenberg. He soon became the Party's leading intellectual, although relatively few members actually ever succeeded in reading his *Myth of the Twentieth Century*, because of its muddled diffuseness. Hitler, however, felt irked by the reputation of a thinker which Rosenberg enjoyed in Party circles. To prove to his supporters that 'the leader' possessed the gifts of the political philosopher in equal measure to those of the practical politician, he determined to write a book of his own.

The outcome of this decision was *Mein Kampf*, the first draft of which had been produced in the congenial atmosphere of Landsberg prison. In contrast to Rosenberg, whose work was full of his own musings on Nietzsche's and Houston Chamberlain's philosophical ideas, Hitler was sufficiently shrewd to dilute the turgidity of *Mein Kampf* with snatches of autobiography. Even so, the personal details he included were, not surprisingly, quite often purely fictitious. He claimed for example to have done well in most school subjects, especially German, whereas in fact Hitler's grasp of his mother-tongue, already adversely commented on in his school reports, had in the meantime shown such scant improvement that the great novelist Feuchtwanger's description of *Mein Kampf* as '164,000 offences committed against German grammar and syntax', was not very wide of the mark. (*Mein Kampf* was nevertheless to achieve a circulation vastly in excess of any other German book for over a decade.)

A much more credible childhood reminiscence quoted in the book told of Hitler's joyful boyhood discovery of a pile of illustrated magazines from the Franco-Prussian War on his father's bookshelves. The pictures and descriptions of battle scenes to be found in those yellowing volumes completely absorbed his interest, as happened later when, during his grammar school days at Linz, he avidly seized on every Boer War report featured in the local papers. As credible as these references to the objects of Hitler's youthful enthusiasms were those that told of his early hates. Vienna was, according to *Mein Kampf*, 'an incarnation of mongrel depravity' on account of its cosmopolitan character. The Jews were 'a pestilence, a spiritual plague infecting everybody—worse than the Black Death'. Socialism was depicted as mob rule exercised over mindless workers by Marxist agitators. As an illustration of this last point, Hitler included an imaginary account of how, during his lean Vienna days, he had been denied the opportunity of earning some money as a building worker, when his refusal to join the trade union had led to his being forced off the site.

Mein Kampf's catalogue of the world's gravest ills, from Jewish pestilence to Socialist mob rule, was only an introduction to Hitler's lengthy prescription for a cure of all these ills. In spite of being repeated at inordinate length, this panacea could be summed up in one word, *Kampf* (struggle), which permeated the whole book from the cover onwards. In his study on the origin of species Darwin had hit upon the 'survival of the fittest in the struggle for existence' as the central factor making for progress and development in nature. Hitler transferred these principles from the field of zoology and applied them to human society. Analogous to the survival of certain species by virtue of their more lethal teeth and claws was the continued existence of races prepared at all times to wage war. A race unwilling to engage in perpetual struggle was forfeiting its right to exist. The Second Reich had been built on blood and iron, but it had been defeated by a treacherous combination of external and internal enemies. If Germany were to be saved and the Third Reich created, an ever more murderous struggle would have to be waged against those forces. Failure to set up the Third Reich by these means would spell the extinction of Germany in a world governed by the inescapable laws of the struggle for existence.

With the first draft of *Mein Kampf* almost finished, Hitler's literary labours were suddenly interrupted by his release from Landsberg jail. As a model prisoner who had given the extremely obliging prison authorities no trouble, he was discharged after serving no more than nine months of his five-year sentence. This is a further striking example of how Kaiser-appointed judges, entrusted with the task of administering the Weimar Republic's law, were treating sworn enemies of democracy.

On his return to Munich and freedom, Hitler had to exchange the role of political philosopher for that of practical politician as a matter of urgency. The Party's stock had slumped during his absence; some of his leading lieutenants had fled the country after the failure of the November *putsch*, whilst those who stayed behind had fallen to quarrelling among themselves as to which of them should assume the functions of the imprisoned leader. All these matters now claimed Hitler's immediate attention.

It did not take him long to arrest the decline in the Party's fortunes. A few wrathful dressings-down, a number of expulsions, and most of his followers fell obediently in line again. Undisputed Führer once more, Hitler could now turn his attention to the crucial issue of deciding along which path the Party should henceforth plan its advance to power: that of legality or of illegality. The march on Berlin by way of Munich had ended in a cul-de-sac; Hitler had no desire of finding himself in the gun-sights of German army rifles again. This resolve was not inspired by cowardice, although the Führer's break for cover as the first shots rang out from the Feldherrnhalle steps had contrasted markedly with Ludendorff's imperturbable advance.

Hitler reasoned thus: the fiasco of the Munich *putsch* stemmed from the unfortunate circumstance that the army and the police had been on the other side of the barricade; this was not to be allowed to happen again. Adventurous short cuts to power, such as the *putsch*, by which the Party was putting itself outside the law, were henceforth ruled out. 'If you can't break them, join them', a saying which was just then gaining currency in gangster-ridden Chicago, exactly sums up what decided Hitler to follow the path of legality after the failure of 9 November 1923.

The success of a revolution of the Right would depend on the attitude of the national classes, the officer corps, the higher civil service, the student fraternities' 'old boys', now holding key positions in industry and commerce. These pillars of German society were not to be alienated by rash adventures. The Party had to switch from lawlessness to surface respectability, from bullets to ballots, if it wanted to impress the classes from which it hoped to draw its future support.

The new respectable front of Nazism at first made little difference to its standing in the country. After the alarums of 1923—foreign occupation of the Ruhr, insurrection in the provinces, collapse of financial credit everywhere—the Stresemann administration had brought about a swift improvement. The Emergency Finance Commissioner, Dr Schacht, had called in the old worthless currency, and issued new *rentenmarks* backed by a mortgage on all land and real estate in the country. The real backing for the new currency, however, was provided by the German public's confidence in it—a novel response elicited partly by the prospect of further American loans and partly by a balanced budget.

Although many Germans, especially of the middle classes, had seen all their savings wiped out by the collapse of the old currency, the inflation had also produced its quota of beneficiaries, among them the national exchequer. The government's internal debt, incurred during the war and aggravated by the costly Ruhr stoppage, was practically wiped out. Other beneficiaries were of the type of the Ruhr industrialist Stinnes, who, assisted by low interest Reichsbank loans, knew so exactly when to buy and when to sell that he made vast profits literally overnight.

Industrialists reinvesting their profits in modernised equipment, public confidence in the mark, balanced budgets, American loans—all these factors combined to set off a business boom in Germany from 1925 onwards. Under such radically altered circumstances the formerly potent appeal of political extremism was bound to diminish. What engaged most Germans' interest in the mid-twenties were such non-political pursuits as earning good money, spending it, enjoying one's leisure time, and so on.

In the course of the prosperous mid-twenties Germany was not only regaining her former economic dominance in Europe (her 1928 iron and steel output figures considerably exceeded those of 1913), she also received diplomatic recognition of her steadily improving status. The 1924 Dawes Plan had provided the Weimar Republic with American loans enabling it to meet revised reparation commitments. And then, in 1925, came the Treaty of Locarno putting an end to the indeterminate relationship half-way between peace and war existing among Germany and the Western powers ever since the Armistice and Versailles. Austen Chamberlain, Briand and Stresemann pledged their respective countries to the goal of peaceful collaboration and the removal of causes of friction. Among the latter the post-war frontiers of Germany had for long loomed quite large. The most important practical aspect of Locarno was therefore Britain's guarantee of the German frontier with France and Belgium, and Stresemann's undertaking that Germany would not seek to revise her eastern boundaries by other than peaceful means. In this way France and Belgium were safeguarded against German revisionism, that is to say the demand for the recovery of Alsace-Lorraine, and Germany was guaranteed against any repetition of the Ruhr occupation in exchange for a promise not to go to war with Poland over the 'Corridor' and Danzig. Stresemann did not, however, state that his country had reconciled itself to the loss of those areas, he merely excluded war as a possible means of recovering them.

At Locarno a new Concert of Europe seemed to be in the making. This process was carried a stage further in the following year by Germany's admission to the League of Nations on whose permanent council she was given a place, as befitted one of the great powers of Europe. Yet beneath the surface amity between the victors and the defeated of the Great War, certain stresses were bound to assert themselves; this was shown by the different interpretations put upon the Locarno arrangements by Stresemann and Briand. To the German statesman they represented the first step towards greater concessions on the part of the Western powers, whilst his French counterpart saw in them the very limit to which his country could go in order to normalise relations in post-war Europe.

In the same year as Locarno another event affecting Germany's political destiny occurred which was equally capable of being interpreted in quite different ways. The Republic's first President, Ebert, died and as his successor the German electorate (by a narrow majority) chose ex-Field Marshal Hindenberg, the hero of the victory at Tannenberg. The choice of the ex-Kaiser's supreme commander for the highest office of state in the Republic at a time of increasing prosperity could not but alarm foreign observers and German democrats alike. But these fears were soon pushed into the background by the new President's impeccably constitutional demeanour, and a radically different interpretation of the outcome of the 1925 presidential elections gained ground: far from undermining the Weimar state, Hindenberg's elevation to supreme office might, in fact, strengthen it by attaching the loyalty of millions of national-minded Germans to the Republic their idol had now agreed to preside over.

One fact was beyond dispute: the army was again, or possibly still, the key factor in German politics; and this, in spite of the limitations on its size and weapons under the Versailles Treaty. The Reichswehr had in fact managed to turn some of the treaty-imposed drawbacks to its own advantage by scrapping obsolete weapons, together with outmoded methods or organisation. It was training its 100,000 members to become a highly efficient nucleus of potentially much larger forces and was carrying out secret research and rearmament projects in such foreign, and as far as the Allies were concerned, uncontrollable countries as Russia, Sweden, Holland and Switzerland.

With the Weimar regime showing signs of stability on so many fronts, economic, diplomatic, political, and even military, the cause of National Socialism could only be advanced with moderate success. The Party was still attracting new members, but the rate of recruitment gave Hitler little cause for satisfaction. Even more irritating to the Führer at this juncture was a bitter controversy with one of his chief lieutenants, Gregor Strasser. One of the few men with ideas of his own ever to occupy an important position inside the Nazi movement, Strasser was determined that the Socialist-sounding items in the Party programme should be more than just catch-phrases. His insistence that Hitler do something about putting those vague slogans into actual practice led to an inter-Party quarrel that threatened to assume sizeable proportions. But this internal wrangle which over-sanguine democrats took to presage the eclipse of Nazism, once again ended in a victory for Hitler. One of the men who, in the course of these polemics, had at first supported Strasser, only to desert him at a crucial moment, was an important new recruit, the Jesuit- and university-trained Josef Goebbels.

Dr Goebbels, an embittered, limping journalist, combined sharp intellect with a vitriolic tongue and immense propagandist ability. His distinctive contribution to the art of propaganda lay in his unerring choice of emotionally charged words—blood, honour, Fatherland, etc.—his insight into psychology and his unbounded cynicism. Typical of these last two aspects was his celebrated remark, 'Any lie frequently repeated will ultimately gain belief'. Hitler appointed him *Gauleiter* (Party district leader) of Berlin. This appointment underlined the fact that National Socialism, hitherto mainly a provincial, south-German phenomenon, was gradually spreading further afield.

During this comparatively static period, the scope of Nazi party activity was expanding in a number of important directions. The Hitler Youth was created under Baldur von Schirach's leadership to cater for youngsters from primary school age upwards. Its long-term purpose was to supply the Party and SA with an ever-increasing supply of suitably indoctrinated recruits. Under the direction of Robert Ley a Nazi rival to the existing trade unions, the so-called German Labour Front, was set up. Its object was the weaning away of organised labour from its Social Democratic, and sometimes Communistic, affiliations. The resulting proliferation of Party operations in varying spheres and throughout many different parts of the country was controlled from the Brown House, the movement's national headquarters at Munich.

Another important innovation introduced in the mid-twenties

was the annual Party rally (the *Reichsparteitag*). This had nothing in common with the annual conferences of other political parties except the name; discussion and voting being anathema to a movement built on the rigid application of the *Führerprinzip* (leadership principle).

The Reichsparteitag was part military review and part marathon mammoth rally. Every event on its programme—march past, trooping of SA colours, torchlight processions, swearing-in of new recruits and mass meetings—was focused on one person: the Führer. Each autumn thousands of brownshirts returned to their homes all over Germany from these annual rallies having been keyed up for another twelve months' campaigning by personal experience of the Führer's spell-binding presence, and by participation in skilfully stage-managed displays involving vast numbers of men. Hitler himself had made the point quite succinctly: 'Mass demonstrations must bring it home to the little man's mind that although he is only a petty worm, he is nevertheless part of a great dragon'.

In the Reichstag elections of 1928 twelve Nazi deputies, among them Goering and Goebbels, were returned, representing a total vote of 800,000 throughout the country. This figure paled into insignificance next to the 9,000,000 votes cast for the Social Democrats, or even the 4,000,000 poll of Hugenberg's Conservative National party. But the fact that after four years of prosperity, Hitler commanded almost as much electoral support as before indicated the measure of Nazism's success. The Party could look upon the hard core of nearly a million voters as the nucleus around which vastly greater numbers were bound to collect should conditions in the country change for the worse. It was in the same year that Stresemann also announced Germany's adherence to the Kellogg Pact, an American-inspired move towards a peaceful utopia. Under its terms the great majority of states in the world pledged themselves solemnly to renounce war as an instrument of policy. In the following year Stresemann accepted the Young Plan for the settlement of the intricate and highly controversial reparations issue within a space of fifty-nine years. Stresemann's acceptance was immediately denounced as a further betrayal of German interests by the government's opponents on the Right. This provided Hitler with the opportunity of launching an anti-Young Plan campaign in conjunction with Hugenberg, the National party leader (and an industrialist and newspaper proprietor of vast influence). Alliance with Hugenberg smoothed the Führer's path appreciably as far as establishing contacts with the captains of Germany's heavy industry was concerned. Contributions by new backers of the steel magnate Thyssen's calibre helped to turn the Nazis into a nationally known alternative to the existing coalition government of middle-of-the-road parties.

On 3 October 1929, Gustav Stresemann died. His death had been precipitated by years of back-breaking exertion in the service of his country's recovery along the path of collaboration with the West. In the last analysis his aim had been identical with that of his bitterest right-wing detractors, for both wanted to see Germany great again. But since a policy of conciliation was bound to yield slower results than one of defiance, Stresemann's entire tenure of office had been accompanied by Nationalist vilification. Three short weeks after the great politician's death, newspaper headlines all over the globe announced the Wall Street Crash. On the Black Friday of October 1929, the world suddenly plunged into what turned out to be the worst economic depression of all time.

5

World Slump and Hitler Boom

FROM ABOUT 1924 onwards the world's economy had shown increasing signs of recovery from the dislocation and depression that had followed the war. This trend had reached a peak by 1929, a year in which all previous productivity records were broken, especially in the United States. By this time production had shot far ahead of actual demand and this, coupled with a spreading fever of get-rich-quick speculation, brought on the Wall Street Crash. There followed the man-made catastrophe of the great depression or slump to whose effects no national economy was immune. It was a crisis of over-production with people enduring hunger not because there was too little food, but because there was too much. This poverty in the midst of plenty lasted into the mid-thirties. Drastic production cuts involving mass unemployment and the destruction of surpluses eventually prepared the way for economic recovery after a slump longer and more terrible than had been known before.

Up till 1929 Germany had been second only to the United States in the speed and scale of economic expansion. A number of factors contributed to this: the Dawes Plan which made large American loans available to Germany, confidence in Schacht's new currency arrangements and the skill with which heavy industry and the large banks had preserved their assets intact during the inflation. Thus there had been no lack of either foreign (largely American) or German capital for investing in Germany's first 'economic miracle'.

This miracle was to end abruptly immediately after Wall Street's Black Friday on which the so-called gold-paved pavements of that famous street were allegedly littered with the bodies of suicidal stockbrokers. American loans and investments in Germany stopped. Demand for her goods dried up simultaneously on all foreign markets and thus of all the world's industrial countries Germany was soon the one most deeply affected by the depression.

She was more vulnerable for obvious reasons. The Kaiser's government had been confronted with an enormous financial problem: what to do about the 164 milliard mark bill incurred during the War? Other belligerent governments had been faced with similar problems. In most instances they had dealt with them by imposing very heavy taxes, but that was not the method adopted in Berlin. Crushing taxation would have made the war too unpopular. The Reich had, instead, raised additional revenue in the form of loans from the German public and had tried to close the still remaining gap between government income and expenditure by putting ever more paper money into circulation. This procedure was fraught with the gravest risks, but according to the war leaders final victory was bound to provide the solid backing, in the form of booty and indemnities from the defeated Allies, which the millions of new paper marks so conspicuously lacked.

Such was the origin of the inflationary avalanche which was to crash down in 1923, speeded on its way by a government bent on avoiding reparation-payments and by business circles profiting from the ruin of others. Buried beneath it were the life savings of millions of middle-class people, small investors and shopkeepers, pensioned civil servants and others. This wiping out of bank balances, obscured by the short-lived boom between 1924 and 1929, was to contribute disastrously to the whole country's eventual loss of political balance.

And now the great slump—dwarfing anything that came before. A vicious circle of credit stoppages, falling demand, production cuts and mass unemployment leading to ever greater stoppages, production cuts and numbers of people out of work.

These are the unemployment figures for Germany from the start of the depression:

September 1929	1,300,000
September 1930	3,000,000
September 1932	5,100,000
January 1933	6,000,000

The last figure corresponded to almost 10 per cent of the total population of 65,000,000, or roughly one-third of all adult males.

The depression was total in its effect: its victims included farmers and shopkeepers as well as industrial workers; 1,000,000 teenagers came out of school to be apprenticed in the dole queues that stretched endlessly outside the labour exchanges. Qualified workers whose skills had survived the inflation—in contrast to the savings of the middle-classes—found themselves on the scrap heap. The German labour movement, one of the pillars of the Republic despite Communist-inspired schisms, was now still further divided into workers and workless.

At the other end of the political spectrum the slump also caused dissension. Gregor Strasser once again urged that the National Socialist party should live up to the second half of its name. According to Strasser's view, the 'anti-capitalist yearnings of the masses' was intensifying and was crying out to be harnessed by Hitler. But the Führer would have none of it. When local Nazi chiefs in Saxony supported a general strike in that province, he personally intervened to enforce a reversal of policy. Strasser was humiliated, but he still remained in the Party, whereas his brother Otto resigned in protest, announcing 'the Socialists are leaving Hitler'.

Hitler's reaction to the Saxon strike and to Strasser's demand for a left about-turn was perfectly consistent. The alliance with Hugenberg's National party had brought him into contact with captains of industry whom he wanted to convince of his party's indispensability in a period of mounting social unrest. In exchange for their political and financial support the Nazi movement would act as a breakwater against the 'Red Tide'. And the Red Tide was literally rising by now. The 1930 elections saw seventy-seven Communist deputies returned to the Reichstag—compared with fifty-four in pre-slump days.

But there was an additional and much more basic reason for Hitler's adamant opposition to Strasser's Leftist ideas. To Hitler the great industrial magnates represented more than a source of potentially vast financial support; they were actual proof of the validity of the Führerprinzip (or leadership principle) which was central to all his thinking. 'The capitalists have worked their way to the top through their capacity, and on the basis of this selection, which again only shows and proves their higher race, they have the right to lead.'

The leaders of heavy industry showed themselves duly appreciative of Hitler's solicitude. They donated large amounts to Nazi election funds, and this despite the fact that in the course of a new political zigzag Hitler had broken with Hugenberg. The campaign against Germany's acceptance of the Young Plan, carried out jointly by the Nazi and National parties, had been a failure for which Hitler now blamed Hugenberg. The National Conservative party had been 'dragging its feet' during the anti-fulfilment campaign, was the burden of Hitler's indignant complaints; this charge enabled Nazi candidates most effectively to outbid their ex-allies in nationalist voting appeal in the 1930 Reichstag elections.

In Hitler's inveterately opportunistic view this broken alliance might, however, soon be worth reviving again. Hugenberg's newspapers and his film company, the UFA, Germany's largest, had helped to make the Führer nationally known. He therefore took care not to let the Nazi-Nationalist rift go too deep. Slump-ridden Germany was now politically in a state of flux and this might create situations whose fullest exploitation would again require an alliance with more conservative right-wingers like Hugenberg.

An important shift had in the meantime occurred inside the government coalition. Ever since the Weimar Constitution had come into force in 1919, the composition of the Reichstag had been such that no single party could command a clear majority. This had necessitated the government of the Republic being carried on by shifting coalitions of the middle-of-the-road parties. There were in fact no fewer than twenty-one different cabinets in Germany between 1919 and 1933. Inside these coalitions, the Social Democrats, with the almost unchanging support of a quarter of the electorate, had always been an important element. Their partners had usually been the Catholic Centre party (on whose 'list' Dr Adenauer had been voted Lord Mayor of Cologne), and the Liberal Democratic party.

Early in 1930 the government, whose revenue was being drastically reduced by the slump, had decided to cut expenditure on its social services. The suggested reductions in unemployment benefits and pensions put the Social Democrat ministers in a

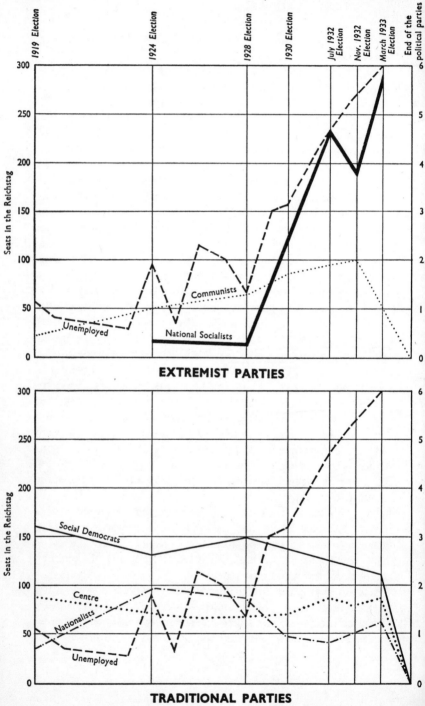

EXTREMIST PARTIES

TRADITIONAL PARTIES

The effect of the Depression on the major political parties

dilemma. As members of the government they realised the urgent need for balancing the budget, but on the other hand they owed it to their working-class supporters to protect their living standards.

This issue divided the Social Democrats sufficiently—similar things were to happen in the British Labour party in the following year—for political initiative to pass to the Centre party. The Centrist Chancellor Bruening put the economy cuts before the Reichstag for its approval—which, however, was not forthcoming. The majority of MPs shrank back from putting their names to such an unpopular measure. At this point the government took a step fraught with the gravest consequences. Ignoring the wishes of the elected representatives of the people, Bruening got the 'economy law' put into force by asking President Hindenburg to use his emergency powers under the Constitution. Hindenburg's signature did the trick; the budget deficit was reduced at the expense of the unemployed and old-age pensioners, but the greatest loser was the cause of German democracy: the will of the majority had been set at naught by the signature of one man.

When the Reichstag protested against this procedure Bruening dissolved it and held fresh elections (September 1930). The results were truly spectacular: an unprecedented political break-through gave the Nazis 107 Reichstag seats in place of the previous 12. The representation of the Communists had increased from 54 to 77. With 143 deputies, the Social Democrats were still the strongest single group, but they had lost votes to their more extreme rivals on the Left, just as Hugenberg's National party had done on the Right.

Greater extremist strength in the Reichstag had its counterpart in spreading political violence outside it. The Nazi storm-troopers were not the only political army existing under the tolerant Weimar Republic; the National party had sponsored the ex-servicemen's organisation of the *Stahlhelm* (steel helmet), and at the other extreme were the 'Red Fighters' of the Communist party. The result was street battles fought out with rifles and machine-guns. The Nazi roll of honour soon included the name of the 'Red Terror' victim Horst Wessel, author and composer of the official party anthem *Clear the roads for the brownshirt battalions*. The opening line of the *Horst Wessel Lied* was clearly inspired by the phrase 'possession of the streets is the key to power'—at that time the most heavily emphasised slogan in the Nazi repertoire.

The police could do little more than reduce the number of armed affrays. Their total stamping out would have required strong government measures going to the very heart of the country's instability. But strong government was the last thing that the deeply split middle-of-the-road coalition could provide in a Reichstag in which it was marooned between powerful extremist blocs both of the Right and the Left.

Bruening tried to redress this internal weakness by efforts designed to produce successes in the sphere of foreign policy. To draw the sting of mounting nationalist agitation at home, he carried on negotiations with Austria for a customs union between the two countries. He also raised the question of a revision of the Polish frontier in Germany's favour. Both these manoeuvres lacked any chance of success in view of France's determination to preserve the settlement of Versailles. They only helped to inflame still further Germany's internal political crisis by pushing the revision of Versailles into the forefront of public attention, a development from which only the extreme Right could derive political profit.

Two ambitious politicians now came forward with divergent schemes of their own for resolving the difficulties in which Bruening had landed the government. The Catholic aristocrat von Papen advised Hindenburg to shift the government's centre of gravity further to the Right by excluding the Social Democrats and admitting the National party. Such a government of the respectable Right, ran Papen's argument, would command the support of all nationally-minded Germans and might well be capable of stealing the Nazis' thunder. Cutting right across Papen's project was the suggestion advanced by General von Schleicher, a professional soldier with political ambitions, that Hitler should be tamed by being invited to share government responsibility.

When the provincial elections of 1931 brought further evidence of Nazi successes (in Brunswick they formed their first Land government, which immediately granted German citizenship to Hitler, up till then an alien and unable to stand for political office), Schleicher thought the time opportune for arranging a meeting between President Hindenburg, Chancellor Bruening and Hitler.

This conference between the ex-Field Marshal and the ex-Corporal ended in disagreement. Hitler had been offered a post in the government in exchange for his promise not to oppose Hindenburg during the forthcoming Presidential election. Convinced that the tide of popular support was still flowing in his direction he refused, thereby denying the 84-year-old President automatic re-election by the combined strength of the middle-of-the-road and the nationalist vote.

Hitler's estimate of his own electoral chances was amply confirmed when 13,000,000 Germans cast their votes for him, a presidential candidate who had never even held office as a town councillor before. Hindenburg received 19,000,000 votes and entered on his second term of office. His first action was the dismissal of Bruening from the Chancellorship. This was done on the advice of General Schleicher who had suggested to the President that somebody more flexible was needed to lead the next government which would have to do a lot of political manoeuvring in order to survive. The wily von Papen was therefore made Chancellor and General von Schleicher himself was made Minister of Defence in what was to be known as the 'Cabinet of the Barons'.

Schleicher's great influence during this period of bewildering zigzags and intrigues derived from his claim to be acting as the spokesman of the army. The army as a political force had kept discreetly in the background since the end of the war, only coming into the open very occasionally, e.g. during the Kapp *putsch* (Berlin 1920), and the Hitler *putsch* (Munich 1923), to throw its considerable weight into the scales on behalf of the government. The civilian government knew the debt of gratitude it owed to the Wehrmacht and consistently abetted its evasions of the limitations on its size and weapons imposed by the Versailles Treaty. Even Stresemann's policy of reconciliation between Germany and the West had been partly motivated by the calculation that greater Western trust of Germany would result in fewer restrictions on her armed strength. In addition, ever since 1922 (Treaty of Rapallo), the Russians had made airfields and factories available to the Germans for the purpose of secret training and weapon production outside the scope of Allied supervision and control.

Schleicher now once again opened negotiations with the Nazis, this time through Captain Roehm, the storm-troop leader, with whom he was personally acquainted. As before, Schleicher aimed at bringing the Nazis into the government, this time for the purpose of giving it the solid support in the country which the 'cabinet of the barons' was lacking. As an inducement, Papen lifted a ban on the military activities of the SA which his predecessor Bruening had imposed. In spite of these blandishments Hitler refused to enter the government on terms other than his own. The relaxation of the ban on the SA led to renewed outbreaks of violence, especially in north Germany where the Left still felt strong enough to challenge the Nazis' 'possession of the streets'. This presented the right-winger Papen with the pretext he had been looking for. He charged the Social Democrat provincial government of Prussia with having failed to maintain law and order and dissolved it. Once again it was a question of using emergency powers under the Constitution to undermine the very democracy the Constitution had been designed to uphold.

The government's continued lack of popular support forced Papen to dissolve the Reichstag in the hope that the elections would show a swing in his favour. The weeks preceding polling day (July 1932), saw the Nazi propaganda machine working at full stretch. Hitler felt that power was now at long last really within his grasp, and strained every muscle to achieve it. He campaigned like a man possessed; possessed both by an insatiable craving for power and the unshakable conviction that he was destined to be Germany's saviour. Conducting an election campaign the like of which the country had not seen before, he flew in his private plane from town to town right round the clock to address monster rallies, day-in, day-out, for weeks on end. By means of this airborne operation for which Goebbels coined the slogan 'Hitler over Germany', the Führer personally put his message before millions of voters.

Nazi election rallies that summer followed an undeviating pattern. The setting was usually a tightly-packed sports stadium draped with swastika flags and slogan-bearing banners. Into the stadium arena would march the serried columns of the storm-troopers to set up their eagle-topped standards to the accompaniment of military marches. Then it was the turn of the local speakers, usually the Gauleiters. These district party bosses, such as Goebbels in Berlin and Streicher in Nuremberg, were effective mob-orators and managed to rouse their audiences to a high pitch of enthusiasm. The drone of an approaching aircraft would impose an expectant silence on the whole gathering. Minutes later the Führer would enter, picked out in the beam of a single searchlight, and advance to the rostrum. There he would pause and in acknowledgement of the crowd's phrenetic cheers jerk his right hand forward in the Nazi salute, all the while keeping his face and body rigidly immobile.

And then suddenly, as if convulsed by a spasm, he would start gesticulating, while words poured from him in a spluttering torrent. Words of derision and boastfulness, of hoarsely bellowing rage and guttural sentimentality. The harsh metallic voice filled the night, driving relentlessly onwards from one peak of audience-echoed frenzy, to the next. His sentences were ungrammatical, but this only stamped them on the minds of his listeners as coming from one of themselves, similarly deprived of the privilege of a good education; the harsh voice, too, struck responsive chords in their hearts. Its metallic ring was a hammerblow against their country's defeat in 1918, and their own personal defeats since, through inflation, unemployment and despair.

The election results showed that the Nazis with 230 Reichstag members representing 13,750,000 voters had become by far the largest party. In fact, never in parliamentary history had any single party managed to attract so much support from the German electorate. And yet they were still some 4,000,000 votes short of the absolute majority which alone could have given Hitler the sort of power on his own terms he had been demanding in his negotiations with Schleicher.

Papen and Schleicher consequently only offered him the Vice-Chancellorship, but he again refused, still convinced that time was on his side. This policy of wait-and-see did not meet with the approval of some of the rasher spirits in the Nazi leadership. The storm-troopers especially were by now spoiling for action and clamouring for their armed 'March on Berlin'. But the Führer remembered Munich. He would countenance no move that might bring him into collision with the army. To attempt a seizure of power now would mean alienating the officer corps, among whom he already had many sympathisers on account of his declared aims of unlimited rearmament. A *putsch* attempt would furthermore frighten off the high state officials on whose administrative ability his own future government would depend. Then there were the propertied classes who might think that a right-wing revolutionary who violated the Constitution would show equally scant respect for contracts and title deeds. And what of the professors, judges, teachers and local government officers, all of whom claimed the deference due to persons of rank because they each individually represented the sublime authority of the state?

No, Hitler would not risk offending the sense of propriety of the respectable national classes. And above all, he felt the need to get the revered symbol of conservative German patriotism, President Hindenburg, on his side. The older and feebler the 'victor of Tannenberg' grew, the more was he becoming the object of a cult among his fellow countrymen.

'I need that feeble-minded old bull,' Hitler told a storm-trooper officer who later deserted him. 'His prestige is still priceless and must be exploited. Here's a symbolic picture I don't intend to miss: the old Field Marshal and the young corporal from the trenches, pledging themselves to the swastika at the court of Frederick the Great. There at Potsdam I'll stage such an act as the world has never seen. With his prestige behind me I'll be able to proceed step by step: I'll get rid of Versailles, I shall rearm. . . . If I force a showdown now the old idiot might resign and that's something I cannot afford. What if the Reichswehr (army) shoot again? No, November 1923 was enough; I've learnt since then. If you can achieve something by cunning don't try noble deeds—you might get your teeth knocked out.' Later in the same conversation, Hitler turned to his plans for the future as far as foreign policy was concerned. 'If it's going to take bombs to show those gentlemen in London and Paris that I mean business—well, they can have them. Don't worry, I'll go to the limit when the time comes, but not before . . . I've learned to wait. . . . I have only one thought: to make Germany great. . . . I can see a German Reich stretching from the North Sea to the Urals, but without Stalin.'

Within the short space of one decade these remarks, expressed in the privacy of a Berlin boarding house, were being translated into practice, word by word.

But in the meantime new problems were to claim Hitler's immediate attention. Fresh Reichstag elections in November 1932 revealed a 2,000,000 drop in Nazi votes, resulting in a loss of thirty-four Reichstag seats, whilst the Communists were still forging ahead and had obtained 100 seats and 6,000,000 votes.

Now that the tide was beginning to turn against the Nazis, Papen deemed the moment opportune for renewing his offer of a Vice-Chancellorship to Hitler, failing acceptance of which he threatened another dissolution so that new elections might reveal an even sharper decline in Nazi support.

Hitler refused to be stampeded by Papen's subtle manoeuvres. Standing pat on his demands for a far greater share of power as the price of his joining, and simultaneously reinforcing, the government, he decided to ride out this, as he saw it, purely temporary crisis.

Once again his luck held. Behind Papen's back Schleicher had been engaged in devious intrigues aimed at unseating the Chancellor for reasons of personal rivalry.

Papen was acutely conscious of his own weakness. As a result of Hitler's refusal to join his government, he still lacked a working majority in the Reichstag. Even the Catholic Centre to which he had once belonged, opposed him. To offset this internal weakness he aimed at a spectacular success in foreign policy. This could no longer be achieved in connection with the reparations issue. In 1931 U.S. President Hoover had brought about a suspension of payments for a year to help Germany in her grave economic plight, and then, at the expiry of the Hoover 'moratorium', a Reparations Conference at Lausanne had finally decided to wipe the slate completely clean. However, there still remained the inflamed issue of disarmament. The Versailles Treaty had expressly designated German disarmament as only a first step towards a general limitation of arms among all nations. So far there had been little sign of French willingness to take further steps, although the Allied occupation of the Rhineland had been brought to an end four years ahead of schedule (in 1930). At the Geneva Disarmament Conference in 1932, Papen accordingly demanded German equality in armaments, and walked out when this was refused. He was prevailed upon to return only on receiving an assurance that Germany would be given equality of status within a security system acceptable to France.

This concession fell rather short of the foreign political success

Papen needed inside Germany to bolster his minority government. He therefore asked President Hindenburg to declare a state of emergency. During the emergency, the government's actions would derive their legal sanction solely from the President's signature. Should there be opposition to such an arbitrary regime the Reichswehr would be called in to enforce compliance.

This last point provided Schleicher with the opening he needed. He warned Hindenburg that the army could not be relied upon to enforce Papen's dictatorial decrees in the face of popular discontent. The President therefore demanded Papen's resignation and asked Schleicher himself to form a new cabinet.

The new Chancellor immediately resumed his predecessor's efforts at bargaining for Nazi support. Hitler allowed these negotiations to be reopened, although he had no intention of accepting any agreement not based on the other side's complete acceptance of his own sweeping demands. Gregor Strasser, who was his intermediary in these talks, grew so appalled at the Führer's dishonest conduct that he resigned from the Nazi party and went abroad. This quarrel attracted a great deal of publicity and created the impression that Hitler's political power was at last on the decline.

This impression was reinforced when Schleicher, after failing to broaden the base of his government by extending it to the far Right, surprisingly turned to the trade unions for support. This daring eleventh-hour scheme for stemming the Nazi tide by an alliance of such apparently incompatible forces as the army and organised labour was, however, stillborn; not least on account of its author's previous reputation for deviousness. Under these circumstances the Chancellor's new emergency programme for tackling some of Germany's worst ills such as unemployment, agrarian depression, and price deflation, availed little. But it provoked furious anti-Schleicher lobbying by Junker landowners close to the President. Their wrath was directed at the Chancellor who had ventured to order an investigation into the circumstances under which state subsidies for uneconomic Junker estates in east Germany (*Osthilfe*) had led to the misappropriation of millions of marks.

Schleicher had fixed 29 January as the date for publishing the findings of the investigation into the affairs of the Osthilfe, but political events were to overtake him.

On 4 January Hitler and Papen had a crucially important meeting at the house of the Cologne banker, Schroeder. Shortly afterwards Hitler resumed contact with Hugenberg, his former partner in the campaign against acceptance of the Young Plan. They jointly drew up a plan for a renewed alliance of the National party and the National Socialists. Together they approached the President's son, Oskar von Hindenburg, whom they asked to act as their intermediary in secret negotiations with his father.

Schleicher who saw himself threatened by this high-powered conspiracy, appealed to the President for permission to dissolve the Reichstag, in the hope that new elections would reveal growing popular support for his emergency programme. Hindenburg refused and thereby forced Schleicher into a position where he could do nothing but resign. The date was 28 January, one day before the intended publication of the Osthilfe Report, which never saw the light of day; for in the meantime matters of far greater moment had been decided in secret conclaves between Hindenburg and von Papen. The aristocratic ex-show jumper suggested—and the President now finally accepted—the type of government coalition which Hitler had been insisting on for years: a cabinet staffed partly by Nazis and partly by 'respectable' Nationalists with the Führer at its head. In this coalition between the traditional and revolutionary Right, the aristocrat Papen offered to serve as Deputy (Vice-Chancellor) to Hitler, the man of the street.

And so on 30 January 1933 Hindenburg appointed to the Chancellorship of Europe's second largest country the man who had started his political career fourteen years earlier as the seventh committee man of an obscure crankish group in a Munich beer cellar.

The same night the vast mass-movement into which this group had grown staged triumphal processions all over Germany, the largest of them in the Unter den Linden in Berlin. Standing at the open window of the Reich Chancellery Hitler took a torchlight salute of his brownshirt army which continued for hours. The endless marching columns roared their triumph to the strains of such stirring tunes as *Deutschland über Alles*, the *Horst Wessel Lied*, and a Nazi marching song with the refrain: 'Today we're masters of Germany, tomorrow of the World'.

The Weimar Republic

When the Weimar Republic collapsed early in 1933 such a total transformation of Germany followed that within months no trace of the regime that had kept Germany going through fourteen difficult years remained. To many people abroad, but also quite a few non-Nazi Germans, this represented an astounding phenomenon. Subsequent historians, on the other hand, who studied the documentary evidence on the Weimar era were surprised not so much by the impermanence of the Republic's achievements as by the fact that it managed to last as long as it did. They stressed this aspect since the foundations of German democracy had been perilously insecure from the start. The Nationalist contention that the Republican system had been imposed on Germany by victorious powers in 1918, was a misrepresentation of the facts, but it nevertheless contained a germ of the truth, since many Germans had accepted democracy not of their own free volition, but in the hope that by doing so they might secure a modification of the armistice conditions. When the terms of Versailles, however, turned out to be not only rather stringent, but also in flagrant contradiction of some of Wilson's Fourteen Points[1] (which had been acclaimed a truly democratic panacea for the problems of international society), democracy soon fell into disrepute among important sections of the German electorate.

It must also be remembered that the transition from monarchy

---

[1] Point 4 had referred to all-round reduction of armaments and Point 5 to impartial adjustment of all colonial claims; Versailles had deprived Germany of most of her army and all her colonies. Britain and France had maintained their armed forces and increased their colonial possessions.

94

to Republic during the crucial November days of 1918 only super-ficially merited the epithet 'Revolution', by which some com-mentators had described it. A revolution presupposes a ruling group being forced from power by organised action from below. Germany's November 'Revolution', by contrast, consisted in essence of little more than the replacement of the Kaiser as head of the state by Ebert on Ludendorff's instigation. This change-over was accompanied and, to an extent, accelerated by strikes and mutinies of left-wing inspiration. But although Ebert was a worker and a Social Democrat, he assumed power not to accom-plish, but to arrest, the incipient revolution. This man who had lost two sons in the war was (and in this he typified his party), above all a believer in order and continuity. 'The social revolution', he said in refutation of the Spartakists' demands for wholesale nationalisation, 'I hate it like sin'. The telephone line between his Chancellery and General Groener's Staff HQ, which was per-manently kept open in the months following the armistice, was the umbilical cord of the infant Republic. Ebert's fellow-Socialist Minister of the Interior, Noske, similarly did not hesitate to employ the extreme right-wing Freikorps in silencing the spokes-men of Social Revolution (e.g. Liebknecht and Luxemburg, killed in January 1919). To some extent, of course, this reliance on anti-Republicans in the avowed defence of the Republic, could be rationalised by invoking the spectre of Bolshevism, but this meant either attaching unwarranted importance to revolutionary stirrings in post-war Germany (for example the ineffectual Munich Soviet of 1919), or exaggerating Russia's strength despite her inability to prevent the suppression of Bela Kun's short-lived Soviet regime in Hungary in 1919. In 1920, it was estimated that various patriotic and right-wing organisations had a total of 300,000 men under arms in different parts of Germany. After the Fehme out-rages, the Ruhr occupation and the Munich *putsch* of the next few years, this anti-Republican shadow army diminished in size and importance, but it remained a reservoir from which the subse-quently growing Nazi movement could draw its officer-cadres.

The Republic's founders also contributed in other ways to undermining the system they themselves had created. To demon-strate the moral superiority of their regime over the Kaiser's, they adopted an incredibly lenient and legalistic attitude to their sworn opponents. Whereas under the Reich anti-monarchists had been discriminated against, the Weimar state staffed its civil service, and above all, the courts, with former Imperial officials of professed anti-republican sentiment. Some of the judges carried their anti-democratic bias to inconceivable extremes. A Nazi who had called the Prussian Minister of the Interior a Jew bastard was acquitted at a Berlin court—the judge ruling that the accused's remark had merely registered the fact 'that the Minister was born of a mixed marriage'.

This does not yet exhaust the variety of factors which caused the steady diminution of the Republic's authority throughout its 14-year existence. Many Germans, accustomed to deriving a heightened sense of their own importance from seeing their head of state, the Kaiser, so highly elevated above the ruck of politicians, suffered in their self-esteem when the resplendent Emperor was replaced by a man of common clay, the saddler Ebert. The Kaiser had been heir to the illustrious traditions of the Hohenzollern dynasty and its army; Ebert, by contrast, represented a system of 'alien' provenance and headed a movement to which millions of middle-class Germans were strenuously opposed.

The developments of the post-war period were such that many Germans increasingly felt the need of compensating for their own diminished sense of self-importance, on account of defeat in war, or peace-time loss of status through inflation, intensified competition for jobs, unemployment, etc., by identifying themselves with a great figure or commanding cause. And since they could discern no positive source of attachment, they turned towards resentful rejection of the system under which they lived. This negative mood was very widespread among the middle classes, a section of the community which saw its standards declining both relatively and absolutely in the 1920s. The shopkeepers and independent craftsmen among them had already been menaced by the competition of department stores and industry in pre-war days. This process had become accelerated by the inflation and the subsequent rationalisation of all large economic units. Now that Germany had lost her foreign-inhabited frontier provinces, her colonies and her previously huge military establishment, there were also fewer posts in the government service available to university graduates. An additional threat to middle-class status was the improvement in

the position of the workers under Weimar, when collective bargaining became the rule in industrial relations, and unemployment
and other new social benefits were introduced. No matter how
ill paid a middle-class person had been pre-war, he had always
been able to boost his self-esteem by looking down on the great
number of people below him on the social scale. With the post-war
advances of the trade unions the old social demarcation lines
seemed to become so blurred that many professional people or
shopkeepers already saw themselves, in their horrified imagination, falling by the wayside to make room for the on-rushing big
battalions of organised labour. The older generation among them
reacted to this situation by negative criticism and nostalgia for the
good old days of the Kaiser, but the younger ones demanded
an active outlet for their disillusionment and frustrations, and
found it by swelling the ranks of Hitler's brown battalions. The
tension between old and young was very much a feature of post-
war Germany. A play typical of the expressionist theatre of the
twenties was called *Parricide*. This 'struggle of the generations'
was transferred to the political plane by Nazism projecting itself
as the movement of youth in contrast to the tired old Weimar
politicians. The attraction exerted by the Nazi party on the student
generation was reflected in the fact that the age of their deputies in
the Reichstag was considerably below the parliamentary average.

Whilst the middle classes were permanently estranged from the
Republic—partly because of its alleged championing of the proletariat at their own expense—the workers' attitude to Weimar
changed subtly as time went on. Having in their great majority
initially identified themselves with the new Republic, the workers
had become disillusioned when it brought them no gains greater
than somewhat enhanced legal and social status, welcome though
such innovations as unemployment relief were. By still mainly
voting Social Democrat in the early 1930s, the labouring masses
were demonstrating their continued allegiance to the Republic,
but in so doing, they were now acting less from conviction than
force of habit. In view of the prevailing mass unemployment and
the Bruening government's cuts in their social services, their lack
of fervour was quite understandable. Although possibly the
greater part of the workers had thus remained prepared until this
late hour to vote, though not to fight, for the doomed cause of the

Republic, appreciable numbers, especially among the unemployed, turned to the more extreme alternatives of Nazism or Communism.

These creeds at opposite poles of the political spectrum had, on two notable occasions during the Weimar era showed signs of abating their mutual hostility. The first of these rapprochements had taken place in the disturbed days of the Ruhr occupation (1923), when the Freikorps thug, Schlagerer, executed by the French for sabotage, had been hailed simultaneously as a fighter against the national enemy (by the Nazis) and against Entente capitalism (by the Communists). The envisaged National-Bolshevik front against the West, however, did not materialise, largely on account of the deep-seated antagonism of the two extremist creeds, but in November 1932, there was a more clear-cut instance of Nazi-Communist collaboration: their joint promotion of a transport strike in Berlin for the purpose of weakening the government. Hitler's fleeting choice of such strange bedfellows had been motivated by the adversity of the moment. He feared that the industrialists might, after his temporary setback at the most recent Reichstag elections[1], transfer their financial backing elsewhere, and decided to shock them into accepting his demands for continued support with the bogey of a Nazi-Communist bloc. The Communist role in this manoeuvre can only be understood by following the tortuous (and, as events were to show, incredibly short-sighted) dialectic of their leadership at a time when they so lost their sense of proportion that they dubbed the reforming Social Democrats Social Fascists, because of their collaboration with the bourgeoisie against the 'Revolution'. Considering the Weimar Republic as little more than a veiled form of capitalist dictatorship, the Communist leaders wanted to hasten the advent of Nazism, so that confrontation with the reality of naked capitalist dictatorship might galvanise the working classes into revolutionary action and the final overthrow of bourgeois society.

The relative rise of Communist strength towards the end of the Weimar era was reflected in the virtual doubling of their Reichstag seats between 1928 and 1932; it also affected the attitude of the bankers and industrialists towards the regime decisively. Whilst these ruling groups had been prepared to co-exist with the Republic in the 1920s, they showed signs of near-panic in the

[1] In November 1932 Nazi voting strength had declined by 2,000,000.

depression of the early thirties. When the anti-capitalist yearning of the masses (to quote Strasser's phrase) assumed the form of 6,000,000 votes for Thaelmann as Communist presidential candidate, they concluded that democracy had failed and stepped up their contributions to the 'drummer', to use Hitler's favourite description of himself at that time.

'The drummer' alerting the indifferent to the Fatherland's peril, 'Germany Awake', the call to arms against the forces of Versailles, 'An End to the System' (i.e. the Weimar system)—these were the major themes in the rising crescendo of Nazi propaganda, underscored with numbing regularity by the strident yell of 'Perish Judah'. The black-red-gold flag of the Republic, heritage of the spirit of 1848, was denigrated as the symbol of national shame, symbolising the three hangmen of Germany: the Black International of the Catholics,[1] the Red International of the Socialists and the 'Yellow' International of the Jews.

By stressing the supra-national associations of those two pillars of the Republic, the Social Democrats and the Centre party, this propaganda effectively associated the Weimar system with foreigners in the minds of many Germans. Even more effective was the identification of the regime with the Jews, since this numerically weak (600,000 out of a total population of 65,000,000), but allegedly all-powerful minority presented a physical target on which the frustrations and hatreds of a society in crisis could be most easily focused. The Jews were a lightning-conductor which such institutions as the Labour movement and the Church could not provide. Regarding the last two the Nazis were primarily concerned with crushing ideas—their adherents were to be suborned by coercion, propaganda and bribes.

In the 'Jewish problem' the Nazis had found the catalyst with which to accelerate the dissolution of the Weimar regime: a process of steady erosion of all liberal and humane values made possible by the accumulated effects of defeat, inflation and mass misery. In this atmosphere many educated Germans became receptive to the teaching of Oswald Spengler, who in his *Decline of the West*, had called for a turning away from the corruption of democracy to the heroic values of the Prussian past. Spengler's assertion that

[1] A reference to the fact that the Centrist leader Erzberger had been a signatory to the Versailles Treaty, and that the Vatican had acted as an intermediary during the secret negotiations preceding the armistice in 1918.

'man is a beast of prey' did not seem so preposterous in a situation where hundreds of unemployed would fight each other to get into job queues outside a factory that had advertised one vacancy. His inversion of Clausewitz's dictum to read that 'politics is the continuation of war by other means' seemed equally reasonable in the context of the street-battles between the brownshirts and their opponents, a typical feature of the Weimar regime in its death throes.

Philosophers less well known than Spengler had counselled the Germans not to look to the past, but to the future. Moeller van der Bruck had told of the coming of the Third Reich, a term not merely to be interpreted historically (i.e. the successor of the Reich of Charlemagne and of Bismarck), but religiously: after the hell of war and the purgatory of defeat would come the resurrection, the true Germanic kingdom.

Relatively few had taken note of those philosophical musings, but their underlying assumptions about the weakness and corruption of democracy, their insistence on force and leadership, were shared by millions. It might be said that the body of German democracy had already turned into a corpse by the time it was taken captive.

6

Start of the Thousand Years

THE CABINET FORMED by Hitler and Papen was a coalition in which the Nazi element was supposed to be effectively hemmed in by the more numerous ministers representing the respectable, conservative Right. Vice-Chancellor Papen, Hugenberg (Economics Minister), General von Blomberg (Defence Minister), Baron von Neurath (Foreign Minister) and some other frock-coated notables of the 'old school' confronted Chancellor Hitler, Goering (Minister without Portfolio and Chief Minister of Prussia) and Dr Frick (Minister of the Interior). But if Papen imagined that he had now managed to pull off the trick which his deposed rival Schleicher had originally attempted, i.e. domesticating the Nazi tiger by fitting it out with a keeper's uniform, he was greatly mistaken. Hitler's capacity for deceit and craving for absolute power were such that the scheming von Papen was soon completely outmanoeuvred, and with him all the other seasoned 'elder statesmen' of the conservative Right.

The new cabinet enjoyed both the President's and the army's confidence, but in the Reichstag it had the backing of no more than 247 out of 583 members. Consequently it became Hitler's immediate task to create a parliamentary majority for himself, a majority he only required in order to put an end to parliament for ever—under the guise of observing the constitutional niceties. He was determined to be seen obeying all the outward forms of legal procedure whilst cold-bloodedly preparing to destroy the very substance of legality.

Using the pliant Papen as his mouthpiece he impressed on the aged Hindenburg the necessity for the immediate dissolution of the existing Reichstag so that fresh elections might produce a more accurate reflection of the new political mood in the country. The President, who had refused the hard-pressed Schleicher this very concession only some weeks earlier, was now quite prepared to grant it to Hitler. He signed a decree dissolving the existing parliament and fixed 5 March 1933 as the date for the next general election.

This gave Hitler just over a month in which to bring about that shift of public opinion required to increase his Reichstag support from 38 per cent to 51 per cent of the total. To this end the Nazis now mobilised all their propaganda resources on a hitherto unprecedented scale. Finance had ceased to be a problem; a subscription list for their election funds was headed by Krupp and the Reichsbank President, Dr Schacht. Propaganda was now no longer an activity of the Nazi party as a voluntary political body; through its control of the government, the Party could fully exploit such powerful means of persuasion as the radio, censorship of the Press and pressure on state employees. The latter form of political blackmail was ruthlessly applied by Goering in the Prussian administration where he purged all Democrats and conferred police duties on the storm-troopers.

The whole Nazi election campaign was marked by unbridled violence, especially when there were clashes with the Communists. The tenor of Hitler's speeches was that only he could save Germany from the Red Tide threatening to engulf her after fourteen years of the Jew-ridden Weimar system that had produced nothing but spineless feebleness abroad and rotting corruption at home. 'All I ask of the German people is this: after you have given the others (i.e. the Weimar politicians) fourteen years, grant us four to show what we can do for the country.' In those days the Nazis publicly propagated the myth that they only wanted full powers for a four-year probationary period, after which they would render account to the electorate and ask for a renewal of their mandate. In private, however, Goering had assured Krupp and other industrialists that this election, which required such financial sacrifices on their part, would be the last one for a hundred years.

And then, just one week before Germany was due to go to the polls, the Reichstag building in Berlin went up in flames. The news broke dramatically in a country gripped by political tension and fear of impending civil war. Banner headlines told the worried

Germans: 'Foreign Communist arrested on scene of crime'; 'Comintern (i.e. Communist International) agent confesses'; 'Arson signals Red Revolution', etc.

What was the truth behind this spectacular act of incendiarism which gutted the interior of the ornate Reichstag building, symbol of a democracy now in its death throes? Some weeks earlier the German police had arrested a certain Van der Lubbe, a Dutch vagrant with previous Communist affiliations, on a charge of fire-raising in the countryside. He had been released, only to be discovered again all alone in the huge Reichstag building, as flames were shooting out of the windows. It must be assumed that he was carefully groomed for this part and for the confession he made immediately afterwards, gravely implicating some Communist leaders. A little earlier that evening SA men are assumed to have entered the Reichstag through an underground passage to scatter a chemical substance with a delayed action effect, and to have withdrawn again, leaving Van der Lubbe behind to be conveniently picked up by the police.

The Reichstag Fire Trial, which after seven months' preparation, dragged on throughout the whole of the following autumn, was not an unqualified success for its Nazi stage-managers. It resulted in the execution of the pathetic Van der Lubbe who babbled incoherently in the dock, but the other main accused, the Bulgarian exile Communist leader Dimitrov, conducted his own defence with such skill that the Nazi judicial authorities, conscious of the world-wide interest aroused by the trial, were compelled to acquit him. Yet this relatively minor setback only occurred near the end of 1933; at the time of the actual burning, Hitler managed to turn it at once to his own maximum political advantage. The Reichstag fire had made the German public deeply apprehensive of an impending collapse of law and order and had thereby prepared it psychologically for accepting Hitler's immediate savage measures for 'safeguarding the state from internal subversion'. Within twenty-four hours of the actual outbreak he had obtained Hindenburg's signature to an emergency decree suspending all the guarantees of individual liberty which had been written into **the** Weimar Constitution. Henceforth no actual or potential opponent of Nazism was safe from arbitrary arrest, brutal torture and even murder at the hands of Goering's police.

These measures inaugurated a week's reign of intensive terror and scarifying propaganda culminating on the day of the ballot. When the election results were announced, Hitler was found to have secured no more than 43 per cent of the total vote. His Nationalist coalition partners had, however, managed to amass the additional 8 per cent required to turn it into an absolute majority. The new government could now lay a valid claim to being the executor of the will of the majority of the German people and could back this claim by producing voting figures arrived at in accordance with the rules of the Weimar Constitution.

Hitler was so determined to observe the letter of Republican legality, whilst stamping out its spirit, that he went to inordinate lengths—lengths which could be described as farcical if they had not been so macabre—to procure the constitutional passage of the all-important Enabling Law. The draft for this law was the only legislative measure he put before the new Reichstag. By its passage parliament would legally dissolve itself and abolish all democratic processes throughout the country by conferring unlimited power upon the Chancellor, i.e. Hitler.

This measure, being a fundamental innovation, required, under the Weimar Constitution, a two-thirds majority to pass into law. As things stood the Hitler-Papen cabinet commanded only slightly over half the votes in the Reichstag.

To overcome this difficulty Hitler did two things. He reduced the over-all number of parliamentary votes eligible to be cast by proscribing the Communist deputies, of whom 81 had been elected (by roughly 5,000,000 voters, in spite of the arrests and beatings up that followed the Reichstag fire). This proscription of legally elected parliamentary representatives derived its constitutional sanction from the emergency decree Hindenburg had signed within twenty-four hours of the fire.

He then made non-committal promises concerning the possibility of a Concordat between Germany and Rome to the Catholic Centre deputies (numbering seventy-three), who swallowed the bait and voted for the Enabling Law. Only the Social Democrats had the courage to oppose the Bill in a chamber surrounded by armed SA, but their protest was drowned in the outburst of cheering which greeted the announcement of the voting figures: 441 for the Bill, 94 against.

Thus Hitler had managed to effect the total suppression of liberty throughout every sphere of national life in an ostensibly law-abiding, constitutional manner. Having achieved absolute power by outwardly democratic means, he moved rapidly to crush every form of potential opposition. The outlawing of the Communist party was followed by that of the Social Democrats. (Hitler had intentionally not banned the Communists before polling day, in order to split the working-class vote. Even at this late stage the Communists and Social Democrats had attacked each other with as much vehemence as the Nazis.) The turn of the Centre came next; they had gained nothing from their spineless compromise over the Enabling Law.

Having carried out complete *Gleichschaltung* (or absorption into the Nazi party) of the whole of Germany's political life, the Nazis moved to take over the trade unions. May Day 1933, was declared a holiday—Day of National Labour—and huge workers' rallies took place up and down the country. Addressing one at Berlin, Hitler announced an ambitious programme of public works as part of the Nazi Four-Year Plan, designed to raise living standards and wipe out unemployment.

On the following day trade union officials in all parts of Germany found their offices occupied by storm-troopers. Many union leaders were arrested, union funds confiscated and transferred with the entire membership into the German Labour Front, led by Dr Ley. This organisation imposed Nazi directives on the whole of industry, uniting both employers and employees in a national partnership in which strikes, collective bargaining and the free election of shop-stewards were abolished, and wage-settlements, instead of being freely negotiated, were imposed by the government.

Goebbels, for whom the cabinet post of Propaganda Minister had been specially created, carried out the complete suppression of independent thought in the arts, literature and the theatre. The media of mass communications such as the Press, the radio and cinema were subjected to total Gleichschaltung. Non-Nazi newspapers were either liquidated or taken over, as were publishing houses.

Hundreds of democratic and Jewish writers, journalists, musicians and scientists left the country to avoid arrest or permanent unemployment. They included Albert Einstein, Thomas Mann, Berthold Brecht, Erich Maria Remarque, Bruno Walter, Otto Klemperer, Kurt Weil and others too numerous to mention.

The German public were, however, far less affected by this mass exodus of eminent artists and thinkers than by the all-embracing experience of living in the dawn of a new era, the early stages of the Third Reich.

Thousands of anti-Nazis disappeared either across the frontiers or into prisons and the newly-established concentration camps. An interlocking apparatus of coercion was set up to liquidate most of the real or imaginary enemies of the regime and to intimidate all potential ones. At its head was the *Gestapo* (or Secret State Police) created by Goering. Its executive organs were Himmler's SS,[1] the black-uniformed élite, creamed off from the SA, and a far more effective instrument of terror than Roehm's turbulent army of storm-troopers.

At the same time, millions, either ignorant of or wilfully indifferent to the sufferings of some of their compatriots at the hands of Gestapo, SA and SS, attended mammoth rallies and torchlight processions or stood in line waving flags and cheering vociferously as the Führer or one of his Gauleiters passed in open Mercedes cars.

But the Nazi leaders were sufficiently skilful to realise that they had to expend at least as much energy on giving the people bread as on giving them circuses. With that aim in view tremendous emphasis was placed on the Four-Year Plan which provided for large-scale state-financed slum clearance, housing programmes, land reclamation, road construction and other projects. The number of unemployed which had stood at 6,000,000 at the beginning of 1933 had been reduced to 2,500,000 by the autumn of the following year and diminished steadily from then on.

One of the methods for absorbing large numbers of workless was the introduction of the Reich Labour Service. This was a form of labour conscription under which all young Germans upon reaching a certain age had to perform compulsory work on the land or at construction sites. During that year they were under military discipline and subject to continuous indoctrination.

Another method of reducing unemployment was the Nazi

[1] *Schutz Staffel* (or protective squad).

practice of confining women to the home, thereby making their jobs available to men. This also fitted in with Hitler's attitude to the role of women in society. According to Nazi teaching a woman's total sphere of activity was summed up in the three Ks: *Kinder*, *Kirche*, *Küche* (children, church and kitchen), attention to the first of which was considered far and away the most important.

This concern for large families was rooted in Hitler's obsession with the alleged danger to Germany's security posed by her much more rapidly increasing Slav neighbours to the east. The 'population explosion' among the Poles and Russians would, in Hitler's view, inevitably engulf Germany unless energetic measures to raise the birth-rate and increase manpower for the country's future defence were immediately taken in hand.

He therefore lost little time in enacting legislation making provision for marriage bonuses, family allowances, prizes to mothers of large families, controlled rents, etc. As a result, Germany's birth-rate, which in common with that of all Western countries had declined markedly during the slump, swung upwards again within a very short while.

Intermediate between the tasks of procreating millions of German youngsters and arranging their ultimate deployment in war was the function of the Hitler Youth. This vast organisation was superficially similar to the Scout Movement. Different sections for boys and girls were in turn subdivided according to age-groups. At that point all resemblance ended. In place of international understanding the Hitler Youth were taught to despise all non-Germans and to look with implacable hatred upon such sub-human species as Jews, Negroes and Gipsies. The organisation arranged hikes through the countryside, sleeping under canvas, camp-fires, etc., but its outdoor games were planned like military exercises, boys were made to undergo a series of strenuous field tests before receiving a dagger in lieu of a proficiency badge, and all orders had to be obeyed unquestioningly and immediately on pain of severe punishment or expulsion. This latter sanction was extremely effective since a boy's progress at school or admission to university often depended on his membership of the Hitler Youth.

Having outgrown the Hitler Youth, the average young German did his year in the Reich Labour Service after which he either joined the Nazi party or one of its subordinate organisations, whether it were the Farmers' League, the German Labour Front, the SA or the hand-picked SS.

At no period of his life was the German citizen outside the sphere of the Nazi movement's direct influence. The whole Reich gradually took on the appearance of a gigantic arena in which over 60,000,000 individuals were marching and counter-marching in strict obedience to the orders of one man. This impression was not very far from the truth; but for the short-lived threat of 'revolt' in 1934, Hitler could justifiably echo, at least during the first ten years of the Third Reich, the words of the 'God-given' King Louis XIV: '*l'état c'est moi*'.

The so-called revolt of summer 1934 was preceded by mutterings against the government which expressed a smouldering discontent at the state of affairs existing one year after Hitler's take-over of power. The source of this agitation was not the circles of the German Left who had opposed Nazism, albeit ineffectively, to the very end, whose spokesmen had disappeared either into camps or exile and whose rank and file had, in the main, succumbed to Nazi bribes or threats; the discontent stemmed from one of the most dynamic pressure-groups inside the Nazi party itself, the leadership of the SA.

The storm-troop commanders, led by their Chief of Staff, Ernst Roehm, felt they had been passed over in the general sharing-out of the spoils of office after the take-over of power. Roehm, who had been invaluable to Hitler both as organiser of his private political army and as his go-between with the Reichswehr generals, had hoped to be appointed Defence Minister in the new government. He intended to transform the small regular army with its aristocratic officer corps into a people's army by fusing it with the much larger SA. Many rank and file storm-troopers, too, were disappointed by the comparative moderation which had accompanied the National Revolution of 1933.

Whilst the pent-up frustrations of the preceding years still seemed to demand radical release, many Germans stood in too much awe of established authority to wish for sweeping changes and readily accepted the looting of Jewish shops and public burning of books as a substitute for revolution. In contrast to this satisfied majority, some storm-troopers were gravely disillusioned. They had probably been among the long-term unemployed and had joined the SA as much for the slogans demanding the take-over of large department stores and the 'abolition of the power of rent and interest' as for the free uniform and weekly expense allowance with which they had supplemented their unemployment benefit.

All these trends within the SA menaced and aroused the strenuous opposition of the men who mattered in the circles around the President, the so-called 'Old Guard of Reactionaries', consisting of military high-ups, Junkers, administrators and landowners. In April 1934 Roehm carried his plans a stage further by publicly echoing the sentiments Gregor Strasser had expressed in response to the 'anti-capitalist yearning of the masses' at the height of the slump. In an intentionally provocative speech, the SA Chief of Staff declared: 'The German Revolution was not merely a Nationalist, but a National Socialist Revolution, with a special stress on the word Socialist. . . .'

Hitler realised that this sort of wildly irresponsible speech-making was endangering the stability of the whole coalition of social and political forces on which his regime rested. Roehm had to be stopped, but how?

At first Hitler tried to buy him off by appointing him Minister without Portfolio in the Reich Government. Roehm considered this purely nominal appointment a totally insufficient substitute for the coveted position of Minister of Defence which remained in the keeping of Hindenburg's nominee, von Blomberg. The SA leader was not the man to accept this rebuff passively; he continued to make pronouncements about the necessity for completing the revolution which had only begun on 30 January 1933.

The 'reactionaries' at whom Roehm's threats were aimed did not under-estimate their import. Vice-Chancellor Papen, acting as spokesman of the Old Guard, warned in a speech at Marburg University: 'There is no up-building among everlasting eruptions. It is time to avoid disturbing the labours of serious men and to silence fanatics.'

Goebbels suppressed reports of this speech inside the Reich because it reflected adversely on the unity of government and Party, but the news leaked out and at his next public appearance Papen was loudly cheered by a large crowd. Soon afterwards Hitler attended naval manoeuvres and met his service chiefs aboard the cruiser *Deutschland*. The contentious Roehm issue which dominated their conversation was, after some hard bargaining, resolved to the mutual satisfaction of both parties. In return for the service chiefs' backing for himself as successor to Hindenburg (who was quite senile by now and not expected to survive the year), Hitler promised to undermine Roehm's position by reducing the inflated strength of the SA.

Although this horse-trading was supposed to have been shrouded in the strictest secrecy, a report reached the outside world and was published in Prague. Roehm was duly alarmed, but allowed himself to be persuaded by Hitler into letting his storm-troopers go on temporary leave pending a high-level conference about the SA's future role in the Third Reich.

This conference was due to take place at Wiessee in Bavaria on 30 June 1934. Before dawn of that day Hitler arrived at the holiday resort in an armoured car, accompanied by units of the SS. Roehm and other SA leaders were dragged out of their beds, charged with treason against the state and summarily executed. SS Chief Himmler was in charge of similar, and simultaneous, operations against local storm-troop leaders in Berlin.

At the same time SS men all over Germany entered private homes and liquidated their occupants according to a black list featuring names of individuals who had at some time or other fallen foul of Hitler. The victims of the so-called 'Night of the Long Knives'—other than the SA leadership—included General Schleicher, Gregor Strasser and von Kahr; the latter's crime consisted of having opposed the Munich *putsch* eleven years earlier. Von Papen escaped liquidation only because of President Hindenburg's well-known regard for him; his two secretaries were shot.

One man, a Munich music critic, was shot because he happened to have the same name as someone else on the list.

All these executions were given blanket legal sanction when the Reich government passed a law three days after the event retrospectively declaring the measures taken on 30 June to crush treasonable attacks, as lawful in defence of the state.

Hitler waited a fortnight before announcing his motives for instigating this bloodbath to the Reichstag and the nation. Roehm and Schleicher were posthumously accused of treasonable contact with the French ambassador and plotting a revolt against the Reich government. These fictitious charges were made to sound more plausible by references to the corruption and immorality of most of the SA commanders. Their notorious practices had for long been the subject of gossip throughout the country—but this was the first time that Hitler had publicly shown any awareness of them.

Concerning the other victims of the purge no explanation was offered, nor apparently demanded by the German public. The average German, far from being perturbed by the events of the 'Night of the Long Knives', heaved a sigh of relief at having been spared the horrors of civil war. The phrase 'the Führer knows best', originally devised as a Nazi propaganda slogan, became a sincerely-held article of faith of millions who were abdicating their powers of reason in exchange for a stake, however small, in the Reich which, according to Hitler, was to last a thousand years.

Hindenburg died in August 1934. His death removed the last feeble barrier against Hitler's exercise of unlimited power. The Führer was immediately proclaimed President, although he never used the actual title which in Nazi nostrils reeked of democracy and the Weimar Constitution. Under this constitution the President had also been titular Commander-in-Chief of the armed forces. Accordingly every German soldier, sailor and airman now had to take an oath which included these significant words: 'I will render unconditional obedience to the Führer of the German Reich and People', a most memorable phrase which has been quoted by the defence in every German War Crimes trial since 1945 to shift the blame from the individual accused.

Unconditional obedience to the Führer was not only exacted from the military arm of the state. By the end of 1934 the Reich government, which had originally included more 'Conservatives' than Nazis, had entirely changed its composition. Vice-Chancellor von Papen had been relegated to the rank of German ambassador in Vienna after his Marburg outburst. Hugenberg had been ousted from the cabinet earlier when he had unsuccessfully opposed the absorption of his Nationalist party by the NSDAP. Von Blomberg, like all other army chiefs, was now in Hitler's pocket both on account of the liquidation of Roehm and because the Nazi-inspired rearming of the country involved an enormous increase in his power. The only remaining non-Nazi of importance was Foreign Minister von Neurath, but his departmental field of competence was narrowed down by the creation of two Nazi party bureaux for foreign affairs, headed respectively by Joachim von Ribbentrop (an ex-champagne salesman and self-styled expert on England), and Party theoretician Alfred Rosenberg, who as a Baltic German was mainly interested in eastern Europe.

The civil service and judiciary had been completely 'cleansed' of all doubtful elements. The latter especially had to conform to such new legal maxims as 'the judge's task is not to do justice, but to annihilate the enemies of National Socialism'—formulated by Reich Attorney Parisius on the anniversary of the setting-up of the special People's Courts. The police, which had initially been mainly managed by Goering, the creator of the Gestapo (or *Geheime Staats Polizei*—Secret State Police), eventually passed completely into the control of Heinrich Himmler, the SS chief. Under him the Gestapo became a branch of the Security Police, headed by the SS second-in-command, Reinhard Heydrich.

Heydrich's immediate competence also extended to the administration of the concentration camps, institutions which during the Nazi era absorbed at first tens of thousands and later millions of victims. Concentration camps were not just an incidental by-product of the Nazi system, they were an integral and essential part of it, and not only by virtue of the huge number of victims involved.

Their purpose in the Nazi scheme of things was threefold. Firstly they were centres in which anti-Nazis suffered torture. Secondly they were ever-present reminders to the rest of the population of the fate in store for them if they failed to conform, and thirdly they were a source of financial profit extracted from slave labour.

Camp inmates represented all sections of German society considered hostile to Nazism on account of politics or religion: liberals, Socialists, Communists, pacifists, Jehovah's Witnesses, and especially Jews. Intermingled with them were criminal elements acting as blockleaders or 'Kapos'; their presence in the camps made attempts at self-help among the prisoners impossible and added demoralisation to the prevalent scourges of camp life such as the constant fear of death, fiendish punishments and backbreaking labour on starvation rations.

Although the existence of the camps was supposed to be a closely guarded secret, the Nazi authorities themselves engineered leakages of information in order to keep a feeling of latent terror alive in the country, and to prove to the steadily diminishing minority of Germans whose critical faculties had not yet atrophied the suicidal futility of opposing the regime.

The indefinite detention of a so-called 'enemy of the, state' required no judicial preliminaries other than the insertion of a person's name on a printed form by a Gestapo official. This stroke of the pen legalised both arrest and detention without trial and time limit. Often the period of imprisonment ended with the detainee's wife receiving through the mail an urn containing her husband's ashes.

Whilst still alive, the concentration camp inmates lived in barracks surrounded by electrified fences. At intervals stood watch-towers on which searchlights and machine guns were mounted. The camps were usually situated near quarries or mines, and after a hard day's work the inmates had to perform barrack-square drill. Real or imaginary infringements of camp discipline (such as failing to tuck in one's blanket correctly at the foot-end of the wooden bunk), involved barbaric punishments. These included flogging with ox-hide whips, hanging from wrists tied behind one's back and solitary confinement in 'bunkers', places in which the SS guards gave vent to their most bestial impulses.

It is estimated that the total number of Germans who passed through concentration camp gates, surmounted by the derisive slogan *Arbeit macht frei* (Work makes one free), during the 12 years of Hitlerism runs into several hundreds of thousands. Even so, it amounts to less than 1 per cent of Germany's population total, which in 1935 stood at 65,000,000.

By contrast the names of 14,000,000 Germans appeared on the central index at the headquarters of the Nazi party. This number signifies that two out of every three male adult Germans were members either of the Party or one of its affiliated organisations. Party membership alone, which in 1933 stood at 3,000,000, was double that figure within a few years. With such a vast organisation at their disposal the Nazi leaders managed to create a political octopus whose tentacles stretched into every locality, no matter how remote or small.

Every tenement had its blockwarden (of whom there were 480,000 in all), who transmitted Party directives to all householders and kept an up-to-date dossier on everybody's contacts, reading habits, chance remarks and response to official appeals.

Above the blockwarden were the cell-leaders (who totalled 92,000), then came the ward-leaders (18,000), and so on up the pyramid at the top of which stood the Führer in lonely eminence. Immediately below him were the thirty-two Gauleiters (Regional Party Leaders), each one an almost absolute monarch in his own province, such as the pornographic antisemite Julius Streicher in Franconia.

Among the affiliated organisations the SA still loomed largest. But their importance diminished as a result of the Roehm purge, and the elevation of the SS (who had grown out of the 12-men-strong personal bodyguard of Hitler in 1925) into the élite formation of National Socialism for purposes both of repression and ceremonial. The SA was, however, numerically still far larger and at first outnumbered the regular army (pegged at 100,000 under the Versailles Treaty) by about ten to one. Before 1933 the storm-troopers' primary function had been the application of unbridled violence to Germany's political life. Now that Germany's political life had withered away, the SA had become somewhat redundant. After the excitement of tavern-brawls and street-battles, they had to accommodate themselves to such tasks as organising flag days on behalf of the NSV (or Nazi Welfare Organisation). Brownshirt stalwarts who had formerly smashed beer glasses over their opponents' skulls could now be seen rattling collection tins for Winter Relief at street corners.

But this deployment of the 'brown battalions' for charitable purposes was only an interlude. They could revert to their original role whenever the opportunity presented itself. In every single anti-Jewish action undertaken before the outbreak of the Second World War the SA provided the essential man-power. Their members stood outside Jewish shops during the Boycott of 1933 threatening to beat up any German who ventured near them. In November 1938 the storm-troopers, reinforced by members of the criminal classes, led the orgy of destruction, pillage, synagogue-burning and beatings-up known as the Crystal Night. A few months later they were also made responsible for the pre- and post-military training of all Wehrmacht recruits.

The SS increased in size and importance throughout the whole period. They could be described as a state within a state. Members were immune from the jurisdiction of the ordinary courts, being answerable only to special SS tribunals. There was a separate military SS (the so-called Waffen SS), independent of the Wehrmacht. Himmler and Heydrich controlled the entire police apparatus and the network of concentration camps, deriving considerable profit from the widespread employment of slave labour.

Anyone wishing to join the SS had to provide documentary evidence of purely German and Aryan descent dating back to 1750. (Heydrich himself had apparently had trouble on that score; the dynamiting of his grandmother's tombstone pointed to a deficient pedigree.)

An SS man wishing to marry had to submit both himself and his marriage partner to a searching medical scrutiny, the object of which was to establish whether their union was likely to produce prolific Nordic offspring. Their children were to be taken care of in special institutions or *Ordensburgen* the purpose of which Hitler had thus outlined to Rauschnigg:

'They will produce a youth that will terrify the world. There must be nothing tender or weak about them. The free and grandiose predatory beast must look out of their eyes. Thus shall I expunge millennia of human domestication.'

This was to be the breeding-ground of the élite of the superrace; its products the aristocracy of the Thousand-Year Reich in which they were to lord it over the ordinary German whilst the ordinary Germans would lord it over all the inferior non-Germans.

As two eminent Nazi lawyers, Schwarz and Noack, had written in their commentary on the 1934 race legislation:

'The cultural level of a people can only be raised in so far as the basic racial nucleus is protected and fostered. . . . These principles have hitherto been acknowledged in the breeding of animals and plants, but it has been overlooked that we humans are subject to the same law of nature'.

7

Watch on the Rhine

THE FOUNDATIONS of the Third Reich had thus been well and truly laid. In addition to following the traditions of Charlemagne's First and Bismarck's Second German Empire, it was, according to the confident Nazi predictions, going to differ from them in one significant respect: Hitler's Empire was going to be eternal. This belief in the immutability of the Third Reich was paralleled by the attachment of almost god-like attributes to the figure of its creator.

'It can be said that the most beautiful thought ever conceived by Germans, a thought that has assumed human shape is called Adolf Hitler. He has enabled the entire nation to be receptive to cosmic emanations for the first time and now that our German people absorb the eternal harmonies ever more intensively they will be able in the decades and centuries to come to order their life ever upwards in accordance with the universe.'

This excerpt from a speech by the Bavarian Minister of Culture, Hans Schemm, was typical of the adulation surrounding Hitler. The most widespread slogan of the period, a slogan endlessly repeated in unison by huge crowds at Nazi rallies, was *ein Volk, ein Reich, ein Führer* (one people, one Reich, one Leader).

As yet the aims expressed in this slogan had only been partly fulfilled. One German Reich under one undisputed leader had already come into existence, but the German people as a whole were not yet one unit. There remained outside the Reich's south-eastern boundaries 7,000,000 German-speaking Austrians who formed their own independent state, as well as 3,000,000 Sudeten-Germans constituting a large minority group inside Czecho-slovakia.

Both post-war Austria and Czechoslovakia had been products of the Versailles settlement. This fact alone would have been sufficient to make their existence an affront to most nationalistic Germans. In 1931, at the height of the depression, the Bruening government had mooted an Austro-German customs union in order to alleviate the effects of the slump. This had been vetoed by France and her allies; the result had been diplomatic humiliation for the German Republic and a steady worsening of Austria's economic position.

If Germany now wanted to take steps in defiance of French insistence on Austro-German separateness, she would need a large army to back up her demands. A large German army had, of course, been expressly ruled out by the Versailles Treaty of 1919. But in the intervening period a number of Allied statesmen had had second thoughts about the equity of denying to Germany the military privileges which they were claiming for their own countries.

Under her Chancellors Stresemann and Bruening, Republican Germany had partially worked her passage back into the comity of nations. At the Disarmament Conferences convened by the League of Nations at Geneva, German delegates had asked for military parity with other powers, pointing out that they alone were permitted no navy or air force of their own and had their army restricted to 100,000 men.

These German demands for arms equality had met with widely different reactions among the Allied governments.

British public opinion was on the whole sympathetic to German claims. Even Lloyd George who had been one of the chief architects of the Versailles system, had come round to the view that Germany had perhaps been too harshly treated, and although he was no longer in office, his views still carried great weight.

The French, on the other hand, had no such qualms of conscience. They were in the unenviable position of having to maintain the Versailles system in face of America's retreat into isolationism and Britain's conscience-stricken insularity. Both those powers were separated by varying distances of water from the mainland of Europe, and were therefore spared the unsleeping apprehension with which France viewed the gradual recovery of her defeated enemy. To keep the 1919 settlement in being in the face of sullen resentment of such vanquished, and therefore revisionist, powers as German and Hungary, France had built up a system of east European alliances (the so-called Little Entente), with Czechoslovakia, Yugoslavia and Rumania, as well as with Poland.

When the German demand for parity in armaments was put forward at Geneva, the French, acutely conscious of their neighbour's larger human and industrial resources, opposed it for understandable reasons.

The divergence between the British and French viewpoints on the question of armaments was finally resolved in a compromise by the autumn of 1933. It was proposed that Germany be granted arms parity after a time-lag of four years. This was the sort of Allied concession which only a few years earlier would have helped the Republican German government to refute the Nationalist accusation of lack of patriotism. It would furthermore have been a welcome sign that the World War's heritage of vindictive suspicion was at last being dissipated.

The reaction of Germany's new leadership to this Allied concession, however, was quite different. Hitler startled the world with the brusque announcement of Germany's immediate withdrawal both from the League of Nations and from its Disarmament Conference. 'For a decade and a half the German people have hoped and waited for the time when at last the end of the war should also become the end of hate and enmity. But the aim . . . seems to be not to give peace to humanity at last, but rather to keep it in a state of everlasting hatred.'

He described the four-year qualification as an insufferable discrimination against the sovereign right of the German people, and announced a plebiscite in which the German electorate would be asked to express its approval, or otherwise, of the steps so dramatically taken.

Von Blomberg and the army chiefs were worried lest the Western powers should take counter-measures to forestall the unlimited rearming of Germany in defiance of Versailles which the Geneva walk-out obviously signified. But the Allies, partly, no doubt, inhibited by a feeling of guilt, did nothing, and Hitler's torpedoing of the Geneva Disarmament Conference, on which the peace-hopes of millions of people the world over had rested, received the enthusiastic approval of the German public; 40,000,000 as against

2,000,000 votes were cast in favour of the walk-out. (At least those were the official figures given by Goebbels.)

One of post-war Germany's greatest grievances had been the loss of German-inhabited territory to Poland and the creation of the so-called Polish Corridor by which East Prussia became an enclave cut off from the rest of Germany. It came, therefore, as a great surprise to the rest of the world when a German-Polish friendship pact—the result of a 'hunting trip' to Poland by Goering —was announced in January 1934. This pact offered Hitler a two-fold advantage: it undermined the French alliance-system in eastern Europe and put the question of Germany's eastern frontier 'on ice' whilst he could probe for weaker spots along Germany's other boundaries.

The Poles' acceptance was based on the self-deluding belief that Hitler was thereby committing himself to an acceptance of the existing German-Polish boundary, which not even Stresemann had been prepared to do at Locarno. An equally powerful Polish motive was her irreconcilable hatred of Soviet Russia. The Warsaw government looked upon the treaty as providing Poland with a new and powerful ally now that her former sponsor, France, was proving unequal to her heavy commitments, as exemplified by French inactivity in face of Hitler's provocative withdrawal from the League.

France's Foreign Minister, Barthou, tried to counter these developments by working towards the gradual entry of Russia into the French alliance system. Russia had every reason to respond favourably to this French initiative as the Nazis' accession to power had ended a decade of amicable Soviet-German relations dating back to the Rapallo Pact of 1922. Hitler had never failed to point out that Communism was a pestilence of which he would cleanse the world, and had written in *Mein Kampf*: 'We put an end to the perpetual German march to the south and west and turn our eyes towards the lands of the east. . . . Destiny itself seems to wish to point out the way for us here. . . . This colossal Empire in the east (i.e. Russia) is ripe for dissolution.'

Stalin in his turn had enthusiastically granted Dimitrov political asylum after the latter's acquittal in the Reichstag Fire Trial. The Soviets were beginning to put anti-Fascism rather than the class struggle and Communism into the forefront of their propaganda.

In September 1934 they announced their adherence to the League of Nations. Soviet Foreign Commissar Litvinov soon became a familiar figure at the Palace of Nations in Geneva from whose rostrum he launched a series of eloquent appeals for the setting up of a system of 'Collective Security', i.e. an international arrangement whereby attacks on the independence of one country would automatically bring all the others to her defence. Litvinov's appeals were specifically aimed at the statesmen of the West whom the Russians wanted to win over to a pact system directed against the spread of Fascism and war.

Whatever the Russians' real intentions in mooting that project, there could be little doubt in 1934 that Fascism was growing stronger and thereby accelerating the drift towards war.

Nowhere was this more obvious than in small, land-locked Austria. Hitler, Austrian-born himself, had already ten years earlier outlined the future relationship between his motherland and Germany in the opening paragraph of *Mein Kampf*: 'The reunion of these two German states is our life task, to be carried out by every means at our disposal. Common blood belongs to a common Reich.'

Talk of blood often leads to its shedding. In July 1934 Austrian Nazis, disguised as members of the security forces, entered the Viennese Chancellery and mortally wounded the Catholic Chancellor Dollfuss. Whilst he was left to bleed to death other conspirators seized the main radio station and broadcast an announcement to the effect that a Nazi government had taken control of the country. The resolution of the remaining Austrian Ministers, led by Dr Schuschnigg, and the loyalty of the army, however, brought about a speedy collapse of the *putsch*. Many of the plotters escaped retribution by seeking refuge in the Reich where they were given accommodation at Munich, but Hitler did little else in support of his Austrian henchmen. This non-committal attitude was largely dictated by Mussolini's promptness in rushing troops to the Italo-Austrian frontier as an earnest of his intention to preserve Austria's independence against German encroachments. The heavily compromised German ambassador to Vienna was hurriedly recalled. In his place appeared ex-Vice Chancellor von Papen, barely recovered from the shock of the 'Night of the Long Knives'. Papen's appointment was a most adroit move on

Hitler's part; by it the Führer at one and the same time rid himself
of a troublesome coalition partner who still enjoyed the senile
President Hindenburg's confidence—and lulled the leaders of
Austria's ruling Christian Social party, among whom Papen enjoyed a high reputation as a fellow-Catholic, into a false sense of
security.

The murder of Dollfuss was followed within three months by
the assassination of the French Foreign Minister, Barthou, and
King Alexander of Yugoslavia at Marseilles. Barthou had just welcomed the King at the beginning of his state visit to France when
they both were riddled by the bullets of a Croat terrorist. Croat
nationalists had complained ever since the foundation of Yugoslavia that the new state was dominated by Serbs from the royal
family downwards. Feeding on the discontent of second-class
citizens, some had formed a subversive movement which was
largely directed and financed by Mussolini, who hoped to benefit
from dissensions in a neighbouring country on which Italy had
territorial demands going back to the end of World War I.

There was macabre irony in Barthou's tragic fate; it had been one
of the objects of his diplomacy to foster an understanding between
Italy and Yugoslavia so that Hitler might be denied the opportunity of exploiting friction between the two powers for his own
ends.

Barthou's successor at the Quai d'Orsay was Pierre Laval. He
continued in his predecessor's attempts at drawing Italy into a west
European pact system within which such outstanding problems as
disarmament could be settled by negotiation. Early in 1935
Mussolini declared himself in agreement with the establishment
of the proposed system and in February Britain, France and Italy
jointly called upon Germany to adhere to it.

Hitler's reaction to this initiative was the announcement (in
March 1935) of the reintroduction of conscription in Germany.
This was accompanied by the statement that the Reich, seeking to
combine peace with honour, was embarking on all-out rearmament. A previous French decision doubling the period of conscript
service to offset the reduced intake of recruits born during the low
birth-rate years of World War I, was dragged in by Goebbels'
propaganda machine to provide a pretext justifying this step.

No such pretext was necessary as far as the German public was

concerned. Cheering crowds of Berliners lined the route at the ·
special conscription day parade which was reviewed by Hitler in
the company of von Mackensen, the only surviving Field Marshal
of the old Imperial army.

There were some Germans, however, who were uneasy at the
prospect that the Western powers might take action to uphold the
Treaty of Versailles which Hitler had so defiantly torn up.

Yet behind a smoke-screen of rigorous diplomatic activity the
intensely pacifist West did nothing concrete to make Hitler stop
in his tracks. A full-scale meeting of the League Assembly was
convened on French initiative; this had been preceded by a
top-level three-power conference of France, Britain and Italy at
Stresa. Both the Stresa and Geneva meetings censured the Reich
government for violating its treaty obligations. The League even
went so far as to set up a committee for the purpose of considering
sanctions against Germany. But in effect all this amounted to little
more than an expression of surface unanimity and certain French
statesmen now decided to supplement the ineffectual procedure of
collective League action by bilateral agreements with individual
countries.

They accordingly caused the current Franco-Soviet negotiations
to be speeded up and managed to score a startling trump by concluding a mutual assistance pact with Russia. This impressive-
sounding extension of the French security system was in addition
underpinned by a Soviet alliance with Czechoslovakia, France's
staunchest confederate in Central Europe.

For a brief period of time in 1935 Germany therefore appeared
isolated, or at least hemmed in by this French system of alliances.
But this impression was misleading. It was only a matter of weeks
before Hitler achieved another spectacular breakthrough, this time
in the field of naval rearmament. The British government, possibly
impelled by an awareness of growing Japanese pressure in the Far
East, made an effort at stabilising the European situation by concluding a Naval Agreement with Germany (June 1935). Under its
terms the Reich's naval strength could be expanded until it
reached 35 per cent of the British establishment. This arrangement
amounted to a British *de facto* recognition of Hitler's right to rearm and was deeply resented by Britain's partners in the Stresa
Front (i.e. France and Italy), whom Sir John Simon (the British

Foreign Secretary) had not consulted during his negotiations with von Ribbentrop.

The whole Stresa Front now began to disintegrate. Mussolini, who saw himself cast in the role of heir to the Roman Caesars had long entertained dreams of imperial conquest. He invaded Abyssinia, where the Italians had suffered an ignominious setback in 1896, so as to carve out an Empire for himself on the cheap whilst the Western powers were preoccupied with the problem of Germany. This unprovoked attack on a peaceful African state aroused world-wide indignation.

The British government, which in June had shown itself so appeasement-minded *vis-à-vis* Hitler, now went to opposite extremes and called for the imposition of sanctions by the League on Italy. Premier Baldwin at the same time also ordered the strengthening of British naval forces in the Mediterranean. This was linked with schemes for denying Mussolini's ships the passage through the Suez Canal, stopping the supply of Middle Eastern oil to Italy, and other measures.

But all these plans came to naught. France was aghast at the inconsistency of Britain's policy which apparently aimed at thwarting the relatively harmless Italian dictator whilst the far more dangerous German one was allowed, and even encouraged, to defy the sanctity of international treaties. At the Quai d'Orsay, this procedure was not only considered mad, but also downright bad. British policy could only result in Mussolini being driven into the arms of Hitler, a development which the latter had been looking forward to for some time. Already in *Mein Kampf* he had referred to Mussolini as his mentor, and to Italy as Germany's natural ally in the struggle against France in the west and the Slavs in the east.

The French government accordingly tried its utmost to prevent the British from putting their anti-Italian measures into effect, whilst the Duce's forces pressed on with the last European colonial conquest in Africa. This inability to back up their solemnly declared intentions further discredited Britain and the League in the eyes of the world. The spear-carrying warriors of the Negus (the Abyssinian Emperor) were defeated by Italian bombs as well as poison gas, and the Führer gained a valuable ally in the Duce. Mussolini stated later that the idea of a Rome-Berlin Axis (a major factor in bringing about World War II), was first conceived in the autumn of 1935.

Nineteen thirty-five had not merely been the year in which Hitler had scored such signal successes in the field of foreign policy as the re-introduction of conscription, the Naval Pact with Britain and the beginning of an Italian alliance. A measure of equally far-reaching internal importance had been the enactment of the Nuremberg Laws by which the inhuman racial theories of Nazism were legally put into practice throughout the Reich. All Jews were deprived of the status and rights of citizenship and mixed marriages between Jews and 'Aryans' were forbidden (Law for the Protection of German Blood and German Honour). Relations between the sexes of the two races were stigmatised as *Rassenschande* (race pollution) and involved punishments of medieval severity, such as sterilisation.

In March 1936 Hitler ordered detachments of the newly-expanding Wehrmacht to cross the bridges across a section of the Rhine, thereby carrying out the re-militarisation of the Rhineland. Once again an important clause of the Versailles Treaty was being violated, and whilst cheering Rhinelanders showered the goose-stepping formations with flowers, there was considerable apprehension among German army commanders. The military strength of the Western powers was, after all, still greatly superior to that of the Reich and they reasoned that an armed conflict provoked by Hitler's latest act of defiance could therefore have only one possible outcome: a German defeat.

Yet nothing happened. The Western powers seemed to be in a state of paralysis. This inability to act in defence of the Versailles settlement was partly due to the widely-held British opinion that the de-militarisation of the Rhineland had been both unjustifiable and unenforceable. In addition members of the British government were haunted by the fear of the incalculable consequences that might arise from warlike measures. Baldwin was convinced that defence against modern air-attacks was extremely difficult— 'the bomber always gets through'. (When war eventually came the authorities anticipated heavier casualties from air-raids during the first week than Britain suffered in its whole course.) Pacifism on the part of Britain was soon matched by internal dissensions in France—caused by the conflicting claims on the national exchequer of the army on one side and the social reformers of the 'Popular Front' government on the other.

For these and other reasons Nazi Germany's daring Rhineland gamble succeeded. Hitler's recklessness had again paid off. He roundly berated his military advisers for their faintheartedness, and drew the conclusion that he had a far sounder intuitive grasp of strategy than the Wehrmacht generals with all their professional training.

Western supineness in the Rhineland issue was also partly the consequence of divided counsels over Abyssinia. Britain's Foreign Secretary, Samuel Hoare, had veered round to the French position in December 1935 and had made an arrangement with Laval, his French opposite number, under which Italy was to be bought off by a Western desertion of the Abyssinians. This cynical Hoare-Laval pact had led to an explosion of public opinion in Britain, and Baldwin had been forced to sacrifice both the pact and its architect on the altar of public opinion.

Anthony Eden had then continued the campaign for sanctions at Geneva and the French had held fast to their 'realistic' attitude. When oil was added to the list of materials member-states were to deny Italy, German coal-deliveries helped Mussolini to overcome his fuel shortage, thus making Italy depend on Germany economically as well as politically.

The growth of friendship between Germany and Italy exposed Austria—the buffer-state separating them, whose continued separate existence in 1934 had largely depended on the movement of Italian divisions to the Brenner Pass—to ever-growing Nazi pressure. Chancellor Schuschnigg, who had succeeded the murdered Dollfuss as head of the Austrian government, could not but be apprehensive of the peril in which an accord between his two mighty neighbours was placing his country. Through Ambassador Papen, he arranged a meeting with Hitler (July 1936), the outcome of which was a deceptively mild-sounding 'Gentlemen's Agreement'. Schuschnigg, who wanted to stave off an all-out Nazi onslaught by offering piecemeal concessions, agreed to amnesty all imprisoned Austrian Nazis (many of them guilty of acts of terrorism and arson), and to accept members of the 'National Opposition', i.e. Nazi sympathisers, into the government. Hitler in exchange recognised the full sovereignty of Austria, a country which both signatories referred to as the 'Second' German state. At the time it was Hitler's intention that Austria should be gradually taken over by its own Nazis from within.

The League had officially abandoned its half-hearted, and consequently futile, sanctions policy against Italy a few days before the Austro-German 'Gentlemen's Agreement'. Clearly the two dictators had a lot to congratulate each other about—and then in autumn 1936 Belgium, suddenly announcing her neutrality, withdrew from the west European security system based on the Locarno Pact. This Belgian defection posed a new threat to the French, but they unaccountably did nothing about continuing their system of fortifications (the Maginot Line) from the German frontier along the Belgian one. It may have been that the French leaders felt reassured on account of a British guarantee at the time of the Rhineland crisis, according to which they could count on Britain's military assistance if France was attacked. They certainly had little reason for feeling secure when surveying the position along France's south-western frontier, for in the summer a large-scale civil war had broken out in Spain (17 July 1936). Spanish army chiefs, led by General Franco, were attempting to wrest control of the country from the Republican government at Madrid. The insurgents, who enjoyed the support of the Catholic Church and the right-wing political parties, were soon in occupation of a large part of Spain. At this juncture Hitler and Mussolini decided to intervene, thereby turning an internal Spanish armed struggle into a limited European war. The dictators' main aims in interfering were firstly the overthrow of a Popular Front (i.e. left-wing democratic) government in a key-state of western Europe, and its replacement by a Fascist dictatorship—and secondly the acquisition of up-to-date military experience by 'expeditionary forces' who were participating in Europe's first major battles since the Great War.

As far as Germany was concerned this experience was to be gained mainly in aerial combat. The Nazi 'Condor Legion' rained bombs on Republican targets including undefended towns and villages, one of which, Guernica, became a by-word for horror throughout the civilised world.

Yet paradoxically, whilst Spain was undergoing the unimaginable ordeal of civil war, Hitler's capital city became the venue of international festivities and jollifications. The summer 1936 Olympic Games brought thousands of competitors and hundreds of thousands of spectators from all over the world to Berlin. They came to a city pulsating with purposeful activity. New buildings, crowded streets, smiling uniformed children, cheering multitudes at the stadium where the Führer shook hands with Olympic gold medallists (and pointedly snubbed the Negro athlete, Jesse Owens, who was racially on the same sub-human level as the Jews)—all this presented the picture of a whole nation confidently facing the future; a nation secure in the consciousness of strength regained, both in the military and the athletic sphere. Foreign visitors who went beyond the sprawling housing projects out into the environs of Berlin, saw a countryside of well-tended fields and farmsteads on which the Reich Labour Service (as well as working parties from the concentration camps) had carried out extensive land reclamation and improvement schemes. The *Autobahnen*, or huge motorways criss-crossing the Reich as a network of straight, wide roads carrying fast-moving traffic, were in the initial stages of their construction as part of Goering's Four-Year Plan. Hitler Youth detachments could be seen route-marching with flying pennants across the heaths and through the forests.

Tourists visiting places of entertainment or seaside resorts would encounter groups of German factory workers enjoying themselves with their families on outings arranged at specially reduced rates by the *Kraft durch Freude* (Strength through Joy) organisation of Dr Ley's German Labour Front.

Such a positive impression of Germany was not confined to sightseers and unsophisticated sport enthusiasts. Political figures of the calibre of Lloyd George, the veteran Labour party leader George Lansbury and the present Duke of Windsor—then Prince of Wales and soon to be King Edward VIII—all returned from Germany with the conviction that Hitler, who had received each one of them personally at his residence in the Bavarian Alps, was leading his country to peace and prosperity.

In October 1936 the Reich recognised the Italian Empire of Ethiopia. Mussolini reciprocated this gesture by formally joining Hitler in the Rome-Berlin Axis. Within a month the Axis powers were joined by Japan in the Anti-Comintern Pact (Comintern: Communist International). Early in 1937 Japan renewed her piecemeal conquest of China, whose valuable Manchurian province she had overrun in 1931.

Thus in 1937 war was an integral part of the world scene in Europe and Asia, whilst Africa was still feeling its aftermath.

Throughout the year, Hitler's speeches reflected and exacerbated this situation. Whilst professing his love of peace, he spoke of the 'justified feeling of national honour existing among those nationalities who are forced to live as minorities within other nations'. This was a pointed reference to the Sudeten Germans and implied a veiled threat to the continued existence of Czechoslovakia. In another speech he demanded the return of the colonies Germany had lost under the post-war settlement, in tones mixing sweet reasonableness with growing irritation.

'What the world shuts its ears to today it will not be able to ignore in a year's time. . . . We shall voice our demands for living room in colonies more and more loudly, till the world cannot but recognise our claim.'

In Austria the amnestied Nazis were openly recruiting members in spite of the fact that only the ruling Catholic party was legally allowed to exist. Their task was made doubly easy by widespread unemployment in the country which they could emphatically contrast with full employment in the Reich (where re-armament and conscription had absorbed all available manpower), and by the semi-official status accorded to their leaders, such as Seyss-Inquart, under the 1936 Berlin Agreement.

The Spanish Civil War was entering its second agonising year. Franco was still advancing, but the forces of the legal government, stiffened by Russian supplies and by volunteers from many countries (the International Brigades) were still managing to avert a rout. The toll in human life was staggering. In view of the flagrant intervention of Germany and Italy in the conflict many people in England and France wanted to see their governments come to the aid of the Spanish Republic. The cabinets of Stanley Baldwin and Léon Blum, however, stubbornly pursued a policy of non-intervention, hoping thereby to contain and localise the conflict; in addition they were averse from being drawn into any concerted action with Russia.

In November 1937, Hitler held a secret conference with five of his most important advisers at the Reich Chancellery in Berlin.

Four of them were soldiers: von Blomberg (War Minister), von Fritsch, Raeder and Goering (the Commanders-in-Chief of the Army, the Navy and the Air Force, respectively). The only civilian present was Foreign Minister von Neurath.

The Führer addressed this select audience for several hours, outlining his familiar version of Germany's overriding problem: her lack of *Lebensraum* (living space). 'There have never been spaces without masters and there are none today; the attacker always comes up against a possessor. The question for Germany is: where can she achieve the greatest gain at the lowest cost?'

He answered this rhetorical question by citing Austria and Czechoslovakia as the predestined targets for Germany's first attack. Yet the real solution of the Lebensraum problem could be achieved nowhere else than in the vast spaces of eastern Europe. 'This problem can only be solved by means of force. . . . Granted that we resort to force there remain to be answered only the questions when? And how?'

Once again he answered his own questions: 'It is my irrevocable decision to solve Germany's problem of space at the latest by 1943–45'.

The date was incorrect, but most of his other predictions were not all that wide of the mark. The leading actor had begun setting the stage for World War II.

8

In the Shadow of War

AT THE END of Hitler's prophetic monologue with its blue-print for aggressive war, two of the service chiefs present ventured to express reservations about the risks the Führer was prepared to incur in his quest for living space. They were the Minister of War and the Commander-in-Chief of the Wehrmacht. Hitler, who increasingly looked to his advisers not for advice, but to provide him with a receptive audience to whom he could reveal inspired flashes of historical insight, was not the man to brook such disloyalty.

Von Blomberg and von Fritsch were consequently dismissed from their posts early in 1938. This removal of Germany's highest-ranking army officers was accompanied by a thorough reorganisation of the entire military command structure designed to make the fighting services completely subordinate to Hitler.

The Ministry of War was abolished; in its stead was set up the *Oberkommando der Wehrmacht* (OKW, or Supreme Command to the Forces) under the control of General Keitel, who was in fact Hitler's military office boy. General Brauchitsch assumed the post vacated by von Fritsch. To make the removal of doubtful elements from important positions really thorough-going, Hitler simultaneously replaced von Neurath at the Foreign Office by Ribbentrop, and Dr Schacht, the Economic Minister, by a dedicated Nazi, Walther Funk.

The 'Conservative' Dr Schacht who now relinquished his cabinet post, and subsequently the presidency of the Reichsbank, had rendered the Nazi state invaluable service. As Hitler's 'financial wizard', he had managed to finance Germany's frantic rearmament programme without upsetting the country's financial balance. He had, however, clashed with Goering, the recently appointed Reich Commissioner for the Four-Year Plan, over the latter's reckless disregard for elementary economic safeguards. Hitler was loath to let Schacht go, but in spite of his stupendous financial skill, the erstwhile 'saviour of the mark' was not the ideal administrator from the Nazi point of view. In an earlier memorandum on German colonisation plans in eastern Europe, he had pointed out that other people were already settled there in large numbers, an objection which Hitler had dismissed as 'humanitarian clap-trap'.

This culmination of the Gleichschaltung process at the beginning of 1938, coinciding with a period of grave Western weakness —Blum's Popular Front government was collapsing in France— gave the Nazis the opportunity for taking a decisive initiative in foreign affairs. Decisive action, as had been foreshadowed in Hitler's secret November address to his service chiefs, was to be directed against Austria and Czechoslovakia, in that order. In the same month Hitler had been told by Foreign Secretary Lord Halifax, that Britain considered Germany Europe's bulwark against Bolshevism and that as far as certain changes desired by Germany were concerned, these might come about with the passage of time, as long as no far-reaching disturbances were caused. In this approach Halifax also reflected the attitude of Prime Minister Chamberlain, who thought that Germany had legitimate grievances over Austria, the Czech Sudeten areas and Danzig. To Chamberlain's way of thinking the arms race was less the product of a sinister German design to dominate Europe than of a lack of genuine understanding among the powers.

In January 1938 police at Vienna discovered documents proving the existence of an Austrian Nazi plot to overthrow the Schuschnigg government. Chancellor Schuschnigg, overstrained by the rigours of combating political subversion as well as deep-seated economic distress for years, saw no other way out of this menacing situation than another visit to Hitler—hoping vainly that he might exact a definite undertaking from the Führer to put a stop to the subversive activities of his Austrian followers. Once again, Ambassador Papen made the arrangements for the meeting. It took place at the Berghof, the Führer's chalet near Berchtesgaden in the Bavarian Alps. The conversation between the respective

Chancellors of Germany and Austria was completely one-sided. Hitler yelled at the distraught Schuschnigg:

'You'll wake up one morning and find us in Vienna, just like a spring storm. After our Army, the SA and the SS will move in, and after them the Austrian Legion (i.e. the terrorists who had escaped after Dollfuss's assassination), and nobody will be able to stop their just revenge. . . . Or do you want to make another Spain of Austria? Do you want to take this responsibility upon your shoulders, Herr Schuschnigg?'

Chancellor Schuschnigg was thus confronted with an impossible choice between resistance which might provoke Hitler into immediately invading Austria with overwhelming forces, and impotent surrender to the Führer's demands—which was tantamount to signing away the independence of his country. He chose the latter and returned to Vienna helplessly committed to carry out the following measures extorted from him by Hitler's blackmail: the Nazi movement in Austria was to be made fully legal; the Ministry of the Interior and the country's police force were to be placed under the control of Seyss-Inquart (the Austrian Nazi leader), and Austria's economy was to be integrated with that of the Reich.

As soon as these terms were made public there was a great upsurge of activity on the part of the Austrian Nazis. Power was now practically within their grasp. In order to seize it they could act against their own government with impunity, secure in the knowledge that Schuschnigg was completely hamstrung.

Hitler was quite satisfied in his own mind that the so-called evolutionary course, i.e. the gradual take-over of the government by Austria's Nazis, would produce the desired results. He ordered the Wehrmacht to call off its preparation along the Austrian frontier, and told some Austrian Nazi leaders who had come to see him, that the Austrian question did not require a revolutionary solution. 'The protocol signed by Schuschnigg is so far-reaching, that if completely carried out, the whole problem will be solved automatically.'

Schuschnigg realised this, too, and with Nazi riots and demonstrations sweeping such important provincial centres as Graz, decided on a last desperate bid to contain the engulfing brown tide.

He made arrangements for a national plebiscite in which all Austrians should declare in a free vote whether they wanted to remain independent or desired union with Germany. Sunday 13 March was fixed as polling day. Early in the morning of Friday 11 March, two days before the appointed day, traffic from Germany into Austria was suddenly stopped. Units of the Wehrmacht had taken up positions all along the frontier from Lake Constance to the Bohemian Forest.

When this information reached Vienna, Schuschnigg knew that the breaking-point had been reached. Seyss-Inquart transmitted to him Hitler's demand that the proposed plebiscite be cancelled immediately. In a futile gesture of appeasement the Austrian Chancellor agreed, only to be confronted with the further request that he hand over all government power to Seyss-Inquart.

At its last meeting, the Austrian cabinet was sharply divided. Some ministers favoured a course of defiance; Schuschnigg, however, obsessed with the fear of provoking a civil war in his own country, decided to abandon the unequal struggle. He broadcast to the nation that he had tendered his resignation and that Seyss-Inquart's Nazi cabinet was taking over. A few minutes later he was arrested on his successor's orders and thrown into prison. (In 1945 he was liberated by Allied soldiers alongside a number of important prisoners of the Nazis.)

The new Chancellor Seyss-Inquart formally requested the assistance of German troops in safeguarding Austria from the non-existent threat of internal disorders. During the night Wehrmacht columns rolled across Upper Austria, Hitler's native province, in the direction of Vienna. Gestapo chiefs Himmler and Heydrich arrived in the capital the following day and supervised the establishment of the machinery for extending the Nazi terror throughout the length and breadth of the country. In the afternoon, Hitler was rapturously welcomed back to Linz, the town he had left on his abortive quest for artistic fame thirty years earlier. He announced the incorporation of Austria in the German Reich—the fulfilment of the vision of *Grossdeutschland* (Greater Germany) which had haunted the minds of men on both sides of the frontier for generations.

Within 24 hours of assuming the Austrian Chancellorship Seyss-Inquart resigned his high office and proclaimed Austria's accession (*Anschluss*) to the Reich. Hitler accepted this self-denying gesture on the part of his henchman with tears running down his cheeks, and slowly continued his triumphal progress towards Vienna, where huge crowds were kept waiting for over a day to catch a glimpse of him. The delay was due to Hitler's dissatisfaction with security arrangements, although the SS and Gestapo worked so thoroughly that within a short while 80,000 Austrian citizens (Catholics, Social Democrats, Jews and others) had disappeared into German concentration camps, many of them never to return.

In Vienna, Hitler addressed a gigantic audience from the balcony of the palace where the Habsburgs had resided whilst he had slept in doss-houses. Amidst phrenetic cheering he announced that the whole of the German people, including their Austrian brothers, were to be given the opportunity of declaring in a plebiscite whether they approved of the creation of *Grossdeutschland* (Greater Germany).

This referendum produced overwhelming affirmative votes throughout the whole of the Greater Reich; nowhere more so than in Austria, where the percentage in favour of the country's loss of independence was 99·75 per cent. Even allowing for Nazi falsification of voting returns, there can be little doubt that the incorporation of Austria into the Reich was highly popular. 'Greater Germany' was an aspiration whose roots were deeply embedded in the history of both countries; the cry for union had been raised again and again, e.g. at Frankfurt in the year of the Revolutions, and twice within living memory (1919 and 1931).

Pre-war Austria had been an imperial power with a population of over 50,000,000. In 1919 she had been reduced to a rump of just over 6,000,000, of whom a third lived in the disproportionately over-sized capital city, Vienna. To the Austrians, the Anschluss meant being part of a large state once again, with all that that implied in terms of political self-esteem and increased economic opportunity. Their post-war economy had in turn suffered the impact of inflation, trade depression and tariff discrimination on the part of neighbouring states (including Nazi Germany). Now everyone would benefit from Hitler's full employment policy with its emphasis on armaments and public works projects. Antisemitism which had been widespread in Austria since the days of

Lueger was an additional factor. The prospect of expropriating Jewish businesses and apartments made many participate in Nazi measures ranging from physical torture to the obliteration of the work of such world-famous figures as Freud, Mahler and Kafka.

The German occupation of Austria had drastically altered the pattern of military power in the heart of Europe. The Reich now had a common frontier with Italy, Hungary and Yugoslavia, on all of whom it could consequently exert far greater pressure, but more important still, it encircled the Czech Republic on three sides, holding its designated next victim in a vice-like grip.

Czechoslovakia had been created at Versailles as one of the Habsburg Empire's succession states in conformity with the Wilsonian principle of national self-determination. But owing to geographical factors this state, which had achieved independence after centuries of foreign domination, was itself troubled from the outset by the existence of substantial foreign minorities inside its borders.

Of those minority groups the largest and most troublesome were the so-called Sudeten Germans; these had for centuries been settled in compact groups near the western frontier and in towns of the interior and now numbered over 3,000,000. They had, in the main, been Pan-Germans in the days when Schönerer had startled the Dual Monarchy with his violent German nationalism. Now they were largely supporters of Hitler and of Konrad Henlein, the local Nazi Gauleiter. Henlein had been receiving a monthly subvention of 15,000 marks from the German Foreign Office since 1935, an investment that was yielding profitable dividends within three years. Czechoslovakia's democratic constitution afforded Henlein and his followers very wide latitude for their agitation. Their original demand for greater minority rights was in time magnified to amount to little short of the cession of the Sudeten areas to the Reich; in other words the break-up of Czechoslovakia as constituted in 1919.

Yet although his country was internally menaced by Slovak separatists, as well as Hungarian and Polish minorities, in addition to this highly organised German Fifth Column, President Beneš seemed in a far stronger position than Schuschnigg had been a few months earlier. The Czech Republic was a viable democracy, possessed the highest standard of living—as well as the largest armaments plant (Skoda of Pilsen)—in the whole of central Europe, and had an indisputably efficient and well-equipped army. The country was, furthermore, linked by defence agreements to France and Russia, the greatest military powers in western and eastern Europe respectively.

But Czechoslovakia also presented by the very shape and form of its national existence a challenge which Hitler considered insufferable. The Republic was the embodiment of Versailles, Slav nationalism and democracy, the ally of France and Bolshevism, a haven of refuge for Jews and others escaping from the Third Reich. Every object of the Führer's unbounded capacity for hatred was present in the state over which Edvard Beneš presided in that year of crisis, 1938.

Less than three months after his annexation of Austria Hitler sent a secret directive to the OKW which included the sentence: 'It is my unalterable decision to smash Czechoslovakia by military action in the near future.'

When the Prague government in its negotiations with Henlein showed itself prepared to go to almost any lengths in order to placate him, Hitler instructed his local Gauleiter immediately to follow up every Czech concession by new and obviously totally unacceptable demands.

As a result of Henlein's manoeuvres and the unceasing Nazi incitement of riots and demonstrations in the Sudeten area, the tension engendered by the German-Czech dispute became unbearable by September 1938. One month earlier, the British government had already decided to send a special envoy, Lord Runciman, to investigate German complaints of Czech ill-treatment of their compatriots, lurid accounts of which were daily put out by Goebbels' propaganda machine. The mere fact of Chamberlain's despatch of Lord Runciman to the 'trouble spots' was a diplomatic victory for the Nazis, for it constituted a tacit admission on the part of His Majesty's Government that there might be some validity in the German charges.

From this initial advantage Hitler proceeded with consummate blackmailing skill. He prompted the Polish and Hungarian governments to lay claim to Czech frontier districts inhabited by their respective co-nationals and thereby further tightened the vice gripping Beneš' unhappy country. A Führer order went out to the

Wehrmacht, instructing it to be in a state of combat readiness by
1 October at the latest.

Some Wehrmacht leaders were gravely perturbed by this and
tried to point out the hazards involved in an attack on Czechoslovakia. But Hitler who had confidently asserted two years earlier:
'I go the way that Providence dictates with the assurance of a
sleep-walker', brushed these warnings aside, dismissing their
professional advice as tales told by old wives with gold-braid on
their collars.

A handful of high-ranking officers were now so alarmed as to
moot vague plans for organised action against Hitler. Little came of
their scheming because of its vagueness; the conspirators were
from the outset inhibited by their realisation that the Supreme
Commander against whom they proposed raising a mutiny enjoyed the unquestioning devotion of most of the army, including
their fellow officers. Nor were there any indications that the
civilian population's attitude to the Führer differed appreciably
from that of the soldiers.

The only concrete result of the tentative plot was the resignation
of the Chief of the General Staff, von Beck. This courageous professional soldier acted in the hope that his gesture would set an
example which other responsible Wehrmacht chiefs might follow.
But there was no response from among the officer corps; the general
public, who might have been shaken out of their complacency by
news of the general's resignation, were not informed of it until
some weeks afterwards, by which time Hitler had gained one of the
greatest triumphs of his entire career at Munich. The magnitude
of this Nazi success made Beck's high-principled action appear
quite unimportant.

Hitler had followed his combat-readiness order to the Wehrmacht with a hate-filled anti-Czech harangue at the Nuremberg
Party Rally, that mammoth festival of Führer worship, which
according to the Nazi creed was an 'annual wedding feast between
the Nazi party and the German people'. The speech resulted in an
immediate worsening of the situation across the border where
ever-bloodier clashes seemed to presage full-scale civil war. To
highlight the gravity of the situation even more effectively, Henlein
and many of his followers now arrived on German soil, posing as
fugitives from Beneš' terror.

Within 72 hours of Hitler's Nuremberg speech, Prime Minister Chamberlain took an unprecedented diplomatic initiative in the cause of peace. The 69-year-old statesman who had never flown before boarded an aircraft to see the Führer at Berchtesgaden so as to discuss with him the possibility of resolving the Sudeten crisis. Hitler, though immensely flattered by the Prime Minister's personal visit, adamantly demanded a plebiscite in the Sudeten areas preparatory to their cession to Germany. 'I am determined to settle this and to settle it soon; I am prepared to risk a world war rather than allow this to drag on.' Having obtained Hitler's assurance that he would take no precipitate action until he had received an answer, Chamberlain flew back to London and immediately initiated a series of Western ministerial conferences. On 18 September he committed Britain to a guarantee of Czechoslovakia in return for French acceptance of the Berchtesgaden proposals. After four days of intensive Western diplomatic activity in Prague, Chamberlain again flew to see Hitler (at Godesberg) to inform him that, as a result of unyielding Anglo-French diplomatic pressure virtually amounting to blackmail, the Czech government had agreed to a gradual transfer of the disputed areas to the Reich. To many people in the West the reversion of the German-speaking Sudetenland to Germany was a belated admission that Wilson's famous principle of the self-determination of nations should also apply to the defeated of the First World War. The liberal English journalist Brailsford, for instance, had written, 'The worst offence of the Treaty of Versailles was the subjection of 3,000,000 Germans to Czech rule'.

But to the Czechs the projected transfer of this territory represented an agonising sacrifice for it meant the surrender of their mountainous border region, a natural defence-line whose loss would leave them helplessly exposed to further aggression. Even so Hitler's wrath was by no means appeased. He countered Chamberlain's peace offering by immediately magnifying his earlier demands. He now wanted his army to occupy the surrendered regions immediately. In actual fact he was furious at Chamberlain's complete submission. The 'cunning appeaser' had deprived him, he was to complain seven years later in the Berlin Bunker whilst pondering the causes of his impending defeat, of the pretext for smashing Czechoslovakia there and then.

The time limit Hitler set for the acceptance of his new demands was 1 October. The British Premier flew back for cabinet consultations in an atmosphere over-shadowed by universal preparations for war; air-raid trenches were being dug in London's parks.

Five days before his time limit was due to expire Hitler spoke in Berlin: 'The Czech State began with a single lie and the father of this lie was Beneš.' He went on to produce a long list of blood-curdling Czech atrocities and expressed his belief that 'the time has come when one must mince matters no longer. . . . For in the last resort Beneš has 7,000,000 Czechs, but here there stands a people of over 75,000,000.' This was the signal for deafening cheers on the part of the huge crowd assembled in the *Sportspalast*, as was the subsequent comparison he drew between himself and his adversary: 'In the Great War whilst Beneš was sneaking about through the world, I as a decent soldier did my duty. . . . The decision lies in his hand—Peace or War. He will at last give the Germans their freedom or we shall go and fetch it for ourselves.'

The next night Chamberlain broadcast to the nation: 'How horrible, fantastic, incredible it is that we should be digging trenches and trying on gas masks here because of a quarrel in a faraway country between people of whom we know nothing.'

This reference to Czechoslovakia, a state created by the Allies less than two decades earlier, as an 'unknown country' was indicative of H.M. Government's attitude to this crisis. The Prime Minister was determined to resolve it in a peaceful manner, even if this involved expedients of a dishonourable nature. He obtained the backing of the French Premier, Daladier, and of the Italian Duce, for a new approach to Hitler. It was suggested that the heads of the four major European powers—the Soviet Union being rigorously excluded—should meet in conference to hammer out a settlement.

Hitler agreed to this new initiative on condition that Chamberlain and Daladier drop their suggestion that Czechoslovakia be represented at talks that were to decide her very existence. And so the Munich Conference opened—36 hours before the expiry of Hitler's time limit—in the absence of Czech delegates. The Big Four agreed that the Wehrmacht was to march into the Sudetenland the following day; confronted with the two Axis dictators'

unyielding belligerency, the Western leaders took it upon themselves to manoeuvre the Czechs into accepting the Munich terms
in the interests of world peace.

The Prague government could do little else than accept the
inevitable. Wild talk of summoning Russian aid came to nothing in
view of Poland's refusal to permit troop-movements across her
territory and the Allied governments' grave warnings against any
Czech action which might precipitate war. Stalin's sincerity in
offering military assistance was rather suspect, anyway, as could be
gauged from his increasing reluctance to support the hard-pressed
Spanish Republic.

The Czech Premier, Syrovy, announced over the radio that his
government was prepared to abide by the terms of Munich. He
spoke in tones of great bitterness: 'We were deserted and we stood
alone'. President Beneš resigned his high office and left the country, which was truncated. The Nazi occupation of large areas in
western Czechoslovakia was immediately followed by frontier
rectifications in the interests of Poland and Hungary further
east.

Chamberlain told cheering crowds at Croydon airport upon his
return: 'We regard the Munich Agreement as symbolic of the
desire of our two peoples never to go to war with one another
again.'

The majority of the British public were as eager to believe that
the Munich Agreement spelt 'Peace in our Time' as the author of
that phrase himself. But a number of important figures in English
public life violently disagreed with Chamberlain. Duff Cooper
resigned his cabinet post in protest and Winston Churchill, then a
Conservative backbencher, declared in the Commons debate on
Munich: 'The German dictator, instead of snatching the victuals
from the table, had been content to have them served to him
course by course. . . . A disaster of the first magnitude has befallen
Britain and France.'

The German public also showed signs of initial relief when the
danger of war was seen to have passed. But this relief soon gave
way to a widespread feeling of nationalistic self-intoxication. The
Reich had gained an appreciable increase in population, area and
resources, but what mattered far more was the fact that it had been
able to enforce its will, not merely on a small neighbour, but on the

greatest powers of Europe, powers which moreover had two short decades earlier dictated peace-terms to a defeated Germany.

Chamberlain's sincerely-held belief that the sacrifice of the Sudetenland would make the Führer more amenable to reason— a belief based partly on wishful thinking and partly on the Premier's utter inability to gauge the workings of a mind so totally outside the compass of his own insular experience—was soon shattered. In a speech early in November, the Führer lashed out violently at the small group inside the Conservative party which opposed Chamberlain's policy; because Churchill, Eden and Duff Cooper had tried to arouse British public opinion to the folly of appeasement, Hitler castigated them as reckless warmongers. Worse was to follow!

An embittered Jewish refugee who had escaped to France shot Ernst vom Rath, third Counsellor at the German Embassy in Paris. On 9 November 1938, within 24 hours of this shooting, a gigantic officially-sponsored pogrom took place in Germany in the course of which SA and SS units, acting simultaneously in all centres of Jewish population, fired synagogues, ransacked shops and rounded up thousands of male Jews for dispatch to concentration camps.

The protocol of a special meeting of Nazi leaders on 12 November, records the following dialogue:

> Goering: How many synagogues were actually burned down?
>
> Heydrich: Altogether 101; 76 were demolished; in the whole Reich there are 7,500 shops that have been smashed.
>
> Goebbels: For all that destruction the Jews will have to pay damages. . . .
>
> Heydrich: Total damage is estimated at several hundred million marks. . . .
>
> Goering: I would have preferred it if you had killed 200 Jews instead of having destroyed so much valuable property.
>
> Heydrich: There are 35 dead.
>
> Goering: I shall issue an edict that the German Jews in their entirety will have to pay the sum of one milliard marks as punishment for their ruthless crimes, etc. That's going to hurt.

The so-called 'Crystal Night' was an important turning point in the Nazi persecution of the Jews. Hitherto a whole range of scattered crimes had been committed against this defenceless minority, but the November pogrom was something much vaster: nation-wide bestial brutality perpetrated before the very eyes of the German public. The fact that there was no outcry inside the country—British Press comment by contrast was unanimous in condemnation—convinced Hitler that his subjects were psychologically ready for the ultimate stage of his 'Solution for the Jewish Question', namely genocide—the murder of an entire people.

The following winter was an anxious one. Lord Halifax, who had succeeded Foreign Secretary Anthony Eden after the latter's resignation at the time of the Austrian crisis, received information according to which Hitler intended to take warlike action in the spring. It was even rumoured that this might take the form of a surprise attack in the West.

But in the event the next victim of Nazi aggression was the rump-state of Bohemia and Moravia. Under the Munich terms the Prague government had been compelled to grant the Slovaks (who inhabited the backward eastern part of Czechoslovakia) their autonomy. The Slovak nationalist leader, Monsignor Tiso now helped Hitler to precipitate a new crisis by demanding complete Slovak independence and secession from the Czech state.

President Hacha, the successor to Beneš (who had gone into voluntary exile), sought to prevent the break-up of his state by dismissing Tiso's regional Slovak government. Tiso thereupon appealed to Berlin for assistance and Hitler, once again threatening war, summoned the aged Hacha to Berlin. The Führer's terms were complete independence for Slovakia and German occupation of the rest of the country. Confronted with these terms and the threat of aerial bombardment Hacha collapsed; medical treatment helped him to recover sufficiently to append his signature to a communiqué 'placing the fate of the Czech people in the hands of the Führer'.

Two hours later, at dawn on 15 March 1939, the Wehrmacht crossed the borders of rump-Czechoslovakia. That evening Hitler issued a proclamation from the Hradschin, the Imperial palace overlooking Prague: 'For a thousand years the Czech territories of Bohemia and Moravia have belonged to the historic living space of the German people'. The key to Europe was in Hitler's pocket.

The occupation of Czechoslovakia was an act of naked aggression totally lacking the justification advanced in the case of Austria and the Sudetenland, which was that the action taken amounted to no more than bringing hitherto cut-off Germans into the Reich.

Chamberlain, whose high post-Munich hopes were thus shattered after such a brief lapse of time, asked at Birmingham within two days of the fall of Prague: 'Is this in fact a step in the direction of an attempt to dominate the world by force?' He went on to warn Germany 'that no greater mistake could be made than to suppose that because it believes war to be a senseless and cruel thing, this nation has so lost its fibre that it will not take part to the utmost of its power in resisting such a challenge if it were ever made'.

The exact direction of the next German challenge became clear within the following week when the Lithuanian government yielded to an ultimatum from Ribbentrop and ceded Memel, a frontier district along the East Prussian border, to the Reich. This in turn exacerbated the situation in Danzig, the Free City which had been internationalised under the Versailles Treaty to prevent it becoming a bone of contention between Poland and Germany. The Nazi cry *Heim ins Reich* (Back to the Reich) was rising ever more insistently in the Free City with the result that the Polish government was growing increasingly apprehensive.

On the last day of March, Premier Chamberlain informed Parliament that H.M. Government had given an undertaking to the Warsaw government pledging full British support to Poland in the defence of its independence and integrity. The French authorities fully identified themselves with this British assurance. The Western powers were thus serving notice on Hitler that appeasement was at an end.

This news threw Hitler into a rage. He screamed: 'I'll cook them (the Allies) a stew that they'll choke on'.

At this juncture Benito Mussolini, the senior of the Axis dictators, chafing under the smart of being made to appear rather insignificant by comparison with his German counterpart, decided to steal some of Hitler's thunder and made preparations for an attack on Albania. This unproductive Balkan mountain region was invaded by Fascist forces on Good Friday 1939, and incorporated into the Italian Empire.

The British and French governments reacted to the extension

of the area of possible conflict by giving guarantees to Greece and Rumania to stiffen their resistance to Axis pressure and negotiated an agreement with Turkey along similar lines.

Hitler's rejoinder to this belated spurt of Allied diplomatic activity was his unilateral cancellation, in a Reichstag speech at the end of April, of both the 1934 German-Polish Pact and the 1935 Anglo-German Naval Agreement. To President Roosevelt of the U.S. who had earlier sent him a message emphasising the horror and futility of war, Hitler replied in the most sarcastic vein: 'I fully understand that the vastness of your nation and the immense wealth of your country allow you to feel responsible for the history of the whole world . . . I, Sir, am placed in a much smaller and more modest sphere.' In effect, he told the American President to mind his own business, thus demonstrating to the world that he was quite impervious to an appeal to reason, even if it came from the leader of the most powerful country in the West.

What of the most powerful country in the East? The relations between the USSR and the rest of the world had run a chequered course. During the period following the Revolution, Russia had been ostracised by the world-community, but she had broken this isolation by means of the Rapallo Treaty (1922) with Weimar Germany. This friendly relationship between the 'two defeated powers' of World War I had been maintained for over a decade right up to the advent of Nazism in 1933. From then on Western public opinion had been split on the issue of relations with Russia. Many influential figures had been quite prepared to welcome Hitler as 'Europe's strong shield against the Red menace', whilst others, mainly of the Left, had wanted to bring about a common front with Russia against the Fascist powers. Then there was a third group, who had visions of killing two birds with one stone by embroiling Russia and Germany in war with each other, a war from which the West would emerge as *tertius gaudens* (the laughing third).

When the system of alliances France had set up after the war started breaking down under Nazi pressure, her government thought of a way out by making a pact with Russia. But this was more impressive on paper than in reality, because a tremendous gulf of suspicion continued to separate the two 'allies'. Even when the Popular Front government of Léon Blum came to power in

Paris as the result of a left-wing election victory (1936), there was little change for the better in Franco-Soviet relations.

Whilst the Spanish Republic was fighting for its very life, the Blum government followed its Conservative British counterpart in applying non-intervention. The Russians, on the other hand, sent some supplies, arms and instructors to the Republicans, thereby partly offsetting massive German and Italian assistance to Franco. At the very same time, however, as Litvinov's campaign for Collective Security at Geneva was beginning to gain some foreign support, the Stalinist purge trials inside Russia turned many people in the West against the idea of a Soviet alliance.

Then came the Munich Pact and the short-lived Western illusion that peace had been bought at the expense of Czechoslovakia. Hitler's renewed aggression in March 1939 had led to Anglo-French guarantees of Polish, Rumanian and Greek independence. Because of rising Nazi clamour over Danzig and the Polish Corridor, Western assurances to the Warsaw government were obviously of the utmost importance. Yet these assurances had very little military significance in view of the fact that there was no direct route of access by which Western aid could reach Poland, other than through the territory of the Reich.

The truth of the matter was that the Anglo-French guarantees to Poland were a dead letter unless Russian backing could be secured. In the spring of 1939 British and French representatives in Moscow accordingly started exploratory conversations with Soviet officials. But these talks made little progress because they were bedevilled by mutual distrust and recrimination from the very outset. The British and French governments and large sections of their electorates were deeply anti-Communist; the excesses of the Great Purge inside Russia, as well as certain incidents in the Spanish Civil War, had only helped to deepen their aversion. The Russians, on the other hand, saw in Western non-intervention in Spain and in the Munich surrender convincing proof that Anglo-French ruling circles were, behind a smoke-screen of 'talks', in reality only concerned with building up Hitler for an attack on the Soviet Union.

In May 1939, Stalin suddenly dismissed Litvinov from the Foreign Ministry and replaced him by Molotov. Although talks between Russian and Western officials were still continuing—in these conversations the Anglo-French response was usually much slower than the Soviet one—Litvinov's disappearance from the international scene indicated a far-reaching change in Russia's foreign alignments. Ribbentrop was fully alive to the significance of the change; because Litvinov had been the moving spirit behind the Collective Security campaign, he had been a principal target of Goebbels' vitriolic attacks. Nazi propaganda had long harped on the theme of an international conspiracy aimed at the encirclement of Germany. Allegedly directed by the Jewish triumvirate of Maxim Litvinov, Léon Blum and Leslie Hore-Belisha (Chamberlain's Secretary of State for War), this conspiracy was supposed to demonstrate how both the democratic West and the Communist East were manipulated by the 'Elders of Zion' for their own ends.

In June the German Ambassador, Count von Schulenburg, established contacts with the new Russian Foreign Minister Molotov. Trade talks were soon followed by informal conversations on political matters. At the same time, the Reich stepped up its campaign against Poland, and physical violence between Germans and Poles flared up in Danzig and the 'Corridor'. Mussolini, whose own preparations for war were far from complete, tried in vain to exercise a moderating influence in Berlin through his Foreign Minister (and son-in-law), Ciano. But Hitler's mind was fully made up to strike at Poland at the earliest possible opportunity. This moment was brought appreciably nearer by the turn Russo-German conversations were taking during August. On 14 August, von Schulenburg told Molotov that Ribbentrop would like to pay a personal visit to Moscow. When the Russians hesitated before committing themselves to a move as decisive as the reception of the Nazi Foreign Minister in the Soviet capital, Hitler intervened with a personal message to Stalin requesting him urgently to accede to Ribbentrop's request.

Stalin agreed, and on 23 August an astounded world received the sensational news that Ribbentrop had arrived in Moscow for high-level conversations with Soviet leaders. In the early hours of next morning the Nazi-Soviet Pact was signed in the Kremlin. Superficially drawn up as a Non-Aggression Pact, under which Germany and Russia pledged themselves to give no assistance to each other's enemies in the event of war, it included secret clauses, unknown to, although widely suspected by the outside world at the time, dividing eastern Europe into clearly demarcated German and Russian spheres of influence.

These clauses implied that Hitler was to have a free hand in western Poland and Lithuania whilst Stalin laid claim to eastern Poland, Latvia, Estonia and Finland—all of them, incidentally, countries included in the Russian Empire before the Revolution.

The Nazi-Soviet Pact sealed the fate of Europe. Hitler now knew that he could hurl his forces upon Poland with a crushing superiority in manpower and armour whilst Stalin held the ring. As for the Western guarantees to Poland, Hitler took France to be of little account in the final reckoning. Concerning Britain, he shared Ribbentrop's conviction that 'effeteness' and lack of preparation would combine to prevent the 'nation of shopkeepers' from fulfilling their treaty obligation.

He accordingly tried to press his advantage by suggesting to Nevile Henderson, H.M. Ambassador in Berlin, that Germany should be given a free hand in Europe in exchange for a Nazi guarantee of the integrity of the British Empire.

Chamberlain rejected this incredibly cynical horse-trading offer out of hand. The Germans then drew up a list of sixteen detailed demands which they wanted the Polish government to accept. When the Polish Ambassador, Lipski, called on Ribbentrop to discuss them, the following conversation ensued:

Ribbentrop: 'Have you the authority to negotiate on our proposal?'

Lipski: 'No' (i.e. the decision rests with the government in Warsaw).

Ribbentrop: 'Then there is no point in continuing the conversation'.

That night the German radio broadcast the sixteen points as an example of Hitler's reasonableness and Polish provocative obstinacy. At the same time a fake attack on the Gleiwitz transmitter in Silesia was carried out by SS men dressed in Polish army uniform. They broadcast a short proclamation, fired a few shots in the air and departed, leaving behind a corpse in Polish uniform. The body was that of a German concentration camp inmate who had earlier been given a lethal injection by an SS doctor.

Next morning the German radio spoke of a whole series of frontier violations by the Poles and instanced the Gleiwitz raid as a typical example; by this time every road leading to the borders was swarming with Wehrmacht Panzer columns. At 10 a.m. of the following day, Friday 1 September, Hitler told the specially summoned Reichstag: 'Last night for the first time, Polish regulars fired on our own territory. Since 5.45 a.m. we have been returning that fire and from now on bombs will be met with bombs. . . .'

He went on to express the hope that the West would not intervene in what was, after all, a strictly internal matter between Poland and Germany. No vital interests of France, and certainly none of Britain, were involved in Danzig and the Polish Corridor.

For the next day or two it seemed as if Hitler had calculated correctly. Official circles in the Western capitals maintained an ominous silence which was capable of various interpretations. Chamberlain at this late hour still hoped against hope that Mussolini might be able to prevail upon Hitler to halt the invasion and to participate in another Munich-style European Conference. This hope proved illusory, and so early in the morning of Sunday, 3 September, Ambassador Henderson delivered a British ultimatum in Berlin: Unless German troops were withdrawn from Poland (where they had been making rapid advances during the previous 48 hours), and all aggressive actions were suspended by 11 a.m. of that day, a state of war would exist between Britain and the Reich.

Military operations continued after 11 a.m.; they were to continue for nearly six years.

9

Blitzkrieg

ALTHOUGH NO SCENES reminiscent of the frenzied enthusiasm which had greeted the outbreak of World War I took place in September 1939, there was no German opposition to the war; a war launched on the most threadbare pretexts and visiting whole-sale destruction upon Poland, a country with whom a treaty of friendship had been concluded on German initiative five years earlier.

The army leaders who during the Sudeten crisis had vaguely talked about arresting Hitler if he started a war, did no such thing. Like everyone else in the Wehrmacht, they implicitly and most effectively executed the orders of the Supreme Commander. Like almost all Germans, they experienced a feeling of intense national pride at the lightning speed of the Wehrmacht's advance into Poland.

The offensive had been planned as a concentric drive towards Warsaw from four directions: north (East Prussia), north-east (Pomerania), south-east (Silesia), and south-east (German-occupied Slovakia). The *Luftwaffe* outnumbered the Polish Air Force so overwhelmingly that most Polish planes were knocked out on the ground; Polish communications were totally disrupted. And yet the Polish Army fought on in the forlorn hope that an Allied attack on Germany's western frontier would be launched in time to save their country from being totally overrun.

Along the German-French border two huge systems of forti-fications—the French Maginot Line and the German Siegfried Line—had been constructed in preparation for the Second World War. With her forces mainly deployed in the east, it could not be considered very likely that the Germans would simultaneously launch an attack on the Maginot Line. Yet the French Commander-in-Chief, General Gamelin, restricted the scope of his military operations to routine patrols along the perimeter of the Maginot fortifications during the crucial days of Poland's desperate defence.

By 17 September, when there could be no possible doubt regarding the final outcome of the unequal struggle, Russian troops started moving into eastern Poland. On the 19th, Hitler made a triumphal entry into 'liberated' Danzig, and on the 27th, after a heroic and hopeless resistance, Warsaw capitulated to the Wehrmacht.

The day after the surrender of the capital, Germany and Russia carried out the new 'Partition of Poland' which had been largely foreshadowed in the Ribbentrop-Molotov Pact of the previous month. Stalin drove a hard bargain, and Hitler, mindful of the fact that in spite of Poland's speedy defeat, he still faced the difficult task of settling military scores with the West, actually yielded more ground than had been originally agreed upon. In addition to eastern Poland, all three Baltic states were now to pass into Russia's possession.

German-occupied western Poland was divided into two parts, the border provinces, with their historic *Volksdeutsch* (German) minorities, were 'forever' incorporated into the Third Reich and the truncated rest of the country—renamed the 'Gouvernement General'—was placed under the absolute rule of Governor Hans Frank, formerly leader of the Nazi lawyers' organisation. Frank's rule was marked by unspeakable atrocities against all Jews, as well as Poles carrying out resistance to the Nazi occupation. Of his measures against the latter, Governor Frank himself said: 'If I were to put up a placard for every seven Poles shot, all the forests in this country would not suffice to produce the paper required'.

In a Reichstag speech of early October, Hitler gloated over Poland's defeat, and in the same breath as expressing his unshakable determination to brook no interference with his reorganisation of eastern Europe, appealed to the West to desist from pursuing a war for which there was no justification. He, after all, did not covet one square inch of French soil, not even Alsace-Lorraine which had been German till 1918, and as for Britain, his attitude had always been one of friendship and understanding.

The governments in London and Paris were not prepared to

accept peace at the price of acknowledging Hitler's right to the territories he had conquered by force of arms and the war in the west continued its uneventful course. There was hardly any military activity on either side. This prolonged lull after the Wehrmacht's lightning war (*Blitzkrieg*) in Poland was variously dubbed *Sitzkrieg* (sitting war), *drôle de guerre* or 'phoney war'.

The Russians in the meanwhile brought pressure to bear on all the countries ascribed to their sphere of influence to effect transfers of territory and the establishment of Soviet bases. Whereas the Baltic Republics of Estonia, Latvia and Lithuania acceded to Soviet requests, the Finns refused outright to agree to frontier-rectifications near Leningrad in Russia's favour.

Stalin abandoned cajolery by the end of November 1939 in favour of warlike action against the obdurate Finns. This winter war from which Hitler kept aloof, although the sympathies of the German public, as well as of the West, were strongly engaged on the side of Finland, produced the remarkable spectacle of the Red Army's inability initially to make any headway against vastly smaller military forces.

Britain and France were sufficiently impressed by this resistance to concert measures for aiding the Finns both materially and with troops. These plans were, however, only capable of execution if transit facilities through neutral Norway were made available. When the Germans received intelligence of this Allied project they reacted most strongly in view of their own war-industry's dependence on shipment of Swedish iron ore, which during the six months of the year when the Northern Baltic Sea was ice-bound could only reach Germany via Norwegian ports.

Allied occupation of Norway could thus jeopardise the Reich's vital war supplies. Hitler therefore, in December 1939, established contact with the Norwegian pro-Nazi leader Vidkun Quisling, who offered to carry out a revolt against the government of his own country. Once in power he would bring Norway into the Nazi camp; Hitler would thus be spared the effort of diverting troops from other theatres of operations to carry out a full-scale invasion.

Whilst these various projects were being elaborated in London, Paris and Berlin, the Finns found themselves compelled by a series of belated, but decisive Red Army successes to make peace with the Russians on the latter's original terms (March 1940). This development made the Anglo-French plans for a Scandinavian expedition redundant, but although Finland no longer offered scope for intervention, the interest of both belligerents in neutral Norway had by now been fully aroused. The Royal Navy had some time previously intercepted a German prison ship in Norwegian territorial waters and had rescued British prisoners of war. The British cabinet on 8 April ordered the mining of Norway's coastal waters to prevent the Germans using them. On the following day Hitler unleashed a surprise attack by sea, air and land on Norway as well as Denmark, two countries who had done their utmost to steer clear of the war and whose traditional neutrality had become a by-word in modern European history.

The Danes surrendered without putting up any resistance. Norway, on the other hand, fought back valiantly, especially, with British help, in the area around Narvik. But by the end of April, the Führer felt so confident of complete victory in the Scandinavian theatre of war, that he issued a Wehrmacht directive ordering preparations for a breakthrough on the Western front to be completed no later than 10 May.

This confidence was not misplaced. The Norwegian king and government had to escape into British exile and the country was placed under the rule of Quisling, whose name soon became a term of abuse applied to any person in an occupied country who collaborated with the Nazi overlords.

The German Navy had suffered appreciable losses during the Norwegian campaign, and although this was to affect subsequent German strategy adversely, Hitler and his service chiefs, General Falkenhorst and Admiral Raeder, had ample cause to be well pleased with their gains, which included safety of the all-important iron-ore supply line from Sweden and the control of Norway's deeply indented Atlantic coast, ideally suited to the establishment of bases for submarine attacks on Britain's vital sea lanes.

The Norwegian campaign had another important result. On 10 May, Chamberlain resigned the Premiership as the result of a parliamentary debate in which he was severely censured over the government's conduct of military operations. Winston Churchill, once the Premier's fiercest pre-war critic, and since the outbreak of war his First Lord of the Admiralty, now replaced him under the most difficult circumstances.

On the same day as Churchill assumed the leadership of Britain, Hitler threw his Panzer columns against Germany's Western neighbours, Holland, Belgium, Luxemburg and France. The plan of campaign had been worked out by General von Manstein with certain embellishments in the Führer's own hand. This blue-print had had to be virtually imposed by Hitler on the General Staff, who had drawn up their own plan which was in fact little more than a revised version of the 1914 Schlieffen Plan.

Whereas the General Staff had envisaged the traditional thrust across northern Belgium towards Paris, the Manstein Plan, which was put into operation on 10 May, aimed at the North Sea coast via Luxemburg, southern Belgium and the Somme Valley. What both plans had in common, however, was a total disregard for the neutrality of Holland, Belgium and Luxemburg. None of the German military planners had any hesitation about inflicting the horrors of the Blitzkrieg upon countries with whom they had no quarrel, and whose only possible offence consisted of their geographical position.

The offensive in the west showed Hitler as an innovator, not only in politics, but also in methods of warfare. Parachutists and glider-borne troops were dropped in the enemies' rear, and the Maginot Line, on which the French had anticipated a head-on attack, was outflanked by highly mobile armoured units. Within five days Dutch resistance collapsed and Queen Wilhelmina, accompanied by her government, escaped to London to continue the fight. After two more weeks, during which the Wehrmacht made staggering advances, came the surrender of the Belgian king, Leopold, and his army. The Belgian government, strongly disavowing the action of their sovereign, crossed to England.

By this time the Panzer columns had reached the Channel coast and had wheeled north in the direction of Calais. Their lightning advance had effectively cut off a large part of the French army as well as the British Expeditionary Force. Hitler now unaccountably ordered a slowing-down of the pace of the armoured columns; this gave the British troops a chance of securing their bridgehead at Dunkirk which was not occupied by the Wehrmacht until 24 June. In the meantime a total of 350,000 Allied soldiers, the great majority British, had been evacuated across the North Sea, albeit at the cost of abandoning all their heavy equipment.

Another thrust had carried the German Army to Paris by 14 June. They found the French capital largely deserted as the consequence of a chaotic mass exodus and occupied it without meeting any resistance. The French cabinet had escaped to Bordeaux and had appointed as its head the aged Marshal Pétain who owed his enormous reputation to the successful defence of Verdun twenty-four years earlier. The council of ministers was divided; the desperate advice of those who wanted to arm the civilian population against the advancing Wehrmacht was negated by the expert opinion of soldiers and the right-wing obsession of certain politicians, whose reaction to France's ordeal had been the formulation of the slogan 'Rather Hitler than Blum'. The Pétain government in consequence decreed that all resistance should cease—a decision for which overwhelming enemy superiority and the choking of all roads leading away from the front with refugee columns seemed to provide incontrovertible justification.

On 22 June, representatives of the defeated French army signed the German surrender terms in the Forest of Compiègne, on the very spot where the German emissaries had accepted the Allied armistice conditions on 11 November 1918. To heighten the drama of the occasion, Hitler had ordered the signing ceremony to take place in the same railway coach as had been used twenty-two years earlier. The coach was accordingly brought out of the Paris museum in which it had hitherto been exhibited as a memento of France's triumph.

Yet there was in all conscience no need for theatrical trappings to heighten the significance of the French surrender on 22 June 1940. Hitler had achieved a triumph unparalleled in the whole of Germany's history. He had succeeded in transforming into reality what he had proclaimed in a thousand speeches since his Munich days as a street-corner orator: the sacred duty of wiping out the national humiliation of 1918 and of tearing up the French-inspired Treaty of Versailles. He had been proved right by events, in spite of the misgivings of the professional soldiers and diplomats, who had counselled caution when he had advocated measures which to them had seemed so reckless as to be openly inviting disaster.

The terms which the French representatives had to accept at Compiègne—although far more onerous than Bismarck's in 1871—were not quite so harsh as had been feared by some circles in

France. Nor were they as harsh as was demanded by Mussolini who now insisted on having a say in these matters, since Italy, after having originally stayed out of hostilities on account of being insufficiently prepared, had finally entered the war against tottering France three days before the fall of Paris.

Hitler explained to his belated co-belligerent the motives underlying his lenient treatment of France. It was fear that the French navy and the French Colonial Empire might otherwise be provoked into continuing the war alongside the British. Churchill had, during the crucial days before the surrender, tried in vain to prevail upon the Bordeaux cabinet to continue the fight—if need be from outside France. Yet so convinced had the French leaders been of the hopelessness of the Allied cause that none had responded to Churchill's call. It had been left to a relatively unknown colonel in the tank corps, Charles de Gaulle, to set up the nucleus of the Free French movement in London.

Hitler's leniency towards defeated France found expression in the continued existence of a nominally independent rump-state in the southern part of the country; this was named Vichy France after its capital and was presided over by Marshal Pétain with the assistance of Pierre Laval, who had been Foreign Minister during the mid-thirties. The northern and western parts of the country— as far as the Spanish border—came under complete German occupation with the Wehrmacht and the Gestapo in total control. The million soldiers of the captured French forces disappeared into overcrowded prisoner-of-war camps. Mussolini was awarded a few border districts in the south-east.

One of the considerations uppermost in Hitler's mind when formulating the armistice terms was how next to proceed against Britain. He considered the neutralisation of the French colonies and the laying-up of the French Navy potentially powerful arguments for persuading these by now completely isolated islands off the European mainland to realise that they had no alternative other than coming to terms with the dominant continental power.

But Britain was not intimidated by all this. In spite of apparently hopeless odds, the British people by their conduct provided irrefutable evidence of the truth of Churchill's proud boast: 'If the British Empire and Commonwealth last for a thousand years, men will still say "This was their finest hour"!'

Hitler waited more than a month before summoning the Reichstag for an important pronouncement. Expressing disappointment at Churchill's perversity in wishing to continue a motiveless struggle, he warned him 'more in sorrow than in anger': 'You ought perhaps for once believe me when I prophesy that a great Empire will be destroyed, an Empire which it was never my intention to destroy or even to harm.' But the Führer intermingled these professions of pro-British sentiment with barbed comments on Churchill's declared intention of continuing the war—if need be—even from Canada. 'The leaders could of course escape to Canada, but the people would have to stay on and suffer.'

This was no empty threat. At the time of this Reichstag speech Hitler, to whom it had become fashionable to refer as the 'greatest general of all ages' in Nazi circles, had already issued his directives for Operation Sea Lion, the projected invasion of Great Britain. But this hazardous amphibious enterprise did not get beyond the planning stage. There were a variety of reasons for this: Hitler was growing apprehensive about the imaginary Russian threat to his rear whilst the greater part of his forces should be tied down in the invasion attempt. A more immediate consideration was the necessity for both the German navy and air force securing mastery of the English Channel to enable large Wehrmacht units to be ferried across.

Of this there could be little certainty. The German navy's earlier losses in Norwegian waters had been such as to make its control of the Channel highly improbable, whilst domination of the air-space above the Channel would depend on the extent to which the German air force could make good the inflated claims advanced on its behalf by the Reich Marshal Goering, founder and Commander-in-Chief of the Luftwaffe.

Impressive proof of its inability to do so was afforded during the subsequent Battle of Britain (July–September 1940), when the 'Few' of Fighter Command, in spite of being heavily outnumbered, shot down so many German planes that the Luftwaffe's aim of destroying the RAF bases in southern England had to be abandoned as impracticable. The Germans then switched from daylight fighter attacks on airfields to night bombing-raids on industrial centres. But it can be said that as from 15 September (the last day of the Battle of Britain), Operation Sea Lion was consigned to the

Future Indefinite as far as Hitler was concerned—although there was always a possibility of it being taken up again as a sequel to the already planned invasion of Russia.

Air raids on British cities continued throughout the winter with the primary objective of reducing Britain to the status of a helpless onlooker whilst the fate of Europe was being decided elsewhere. Although under the terms of their pact Hitler had given Stalin a free hand in eastern Europe, Soviet annexation of the three Baltic states and of the Rumanian border provinces of Bukowina and Bessarabia had not really suited Germany's design of establishing her own preponderance in Europe. Hitler had retaliated by strengthening his grip on Yugoslavia, Hungary, Rumania and Bulgaria, a task facilitated by the fact that all these adjacent countries were under semi-Fascist dictatorship and had outstanding territorial claims upon their neighbours. The reciprocal irredentist designs of these Balkan states gave the Nazis a powerful lever for playing them off against each other.

There was a further deterioration in Nazi-Soviet relations as the result of Molotov's visit to Berlin in November 1940. Because an RAF raid was in progress at the time, the Russian Foreign Minister was forced to spend some hours sheltering underground in the company of Ribbentrop. When in the course of the political horse-trading that passed for diplomacy in Russo-German relations, Ribbentrop smugly assured him that Britain was finished, Molotov retorted pointedly: 'If that is so, why are we in this shelter and whose are the bombs which are falling?'

Some time before that the war had been extended not merely to a new front, but to a new continent, when Italian forces based on Libya had advanced into British-held Egypt. This was done partly to offset Italy's undistinguished conduct during the fall of France; in addition, Mussolini had long laid claim to most of the area around the Mediterranean Sea (the *Mare Nostrum* of the Ancient Romans). He may well have imagined himself as following in Caesar's footsteps when embarking on this campaign. But his North African thrust soon spent itself and to distract attention from one fiasco, the Duce in November embarked on another: the invasion of Greece from Italian bases in Albania.

The Greeks, led by General Metaxas, put up a surprisingly successful resistance to numerically stronger Italian forces, and

Mussolini, who had originally launched both the Egyptian and the Greek invasions partly to steal some of Hitler's limelight, soon saw himself compelled to request his Axis partner's assistance in disentangling himself from his difficulties.

The Duce's need of German assistance became more imperative as winter wore on and General Wavell chased the Italians right out of Egypt and across Libya—whilst General Metaxas drove them out of northern Greece into Albania. As a consequence of these unexpected reverses, Hitler was now confronted with the necessity of co-ordinating two divergent strategies: preparations for his long-projected attack on Russia and measures designed to extricate Mussolini from his predicaments in the Balkans and North Africa.

He proved equal to the occasion. Making Greece his first priority, he put pressure on all the countries separating it from the Reich to grant the Wehrmacht transit facilities and the right to establish bases. All four governments involved—Admiral Horthy's in Hungary, General Antonescu's in Rumania, King Boris's in Bulgaria, and Prince Regent Paul's in Yugoslavia—acceded to the German requests. In consequence all the countries concerned, except one, were speedily occupied by Wehrmacht units.

The exception was Yugoslavia, where the government's surrender to the Nazi demands brought about a patriotic revolt led by high-ranking army officers. Their *coup d'état* of 26 March 1940 aligned Yugoslavia alongside Greece and Britain in foolhardy defiance of the Axis Powers. Ten days later Hitler loosed the Wehrmacht and the Luftwaffe simultaneously upon Yugoslavia and Greece. Belgrade, the centre of the patriotic officers' revolt, was singled out for special punishment. Successive waves of Nazi dive-bombers flattened large areas of the defenceless Yugoslav capital and killed 17,000 of its civilian inhabitants in the process.

Within two weeks Hitler's Balkan War was carried to its successful conclusion. Yugoslavia was broken up into various zones, some under German, others under Italian occupation. Conditions in German-occupied Serbia after eighteen months of Nazi rule are reflected in this order of a local Wehrmacht commander (Infantry-General Boehme): 'For every murdered German soldier, a hundred prisoners or hostages are to be taken, for every injured German soldier, fifty prisoners or hostages'.

A similar fate befell Greece where the swastika flag was run up on the Acropolis, ageless symbol of European civilisation. From the North Cape to Cape Matapan the Continent was now entirely dominated by Hitler, although there were still a number of neutral states, such as Spain, Switzerland and Sweden, but their neutrality often operated in Germany's favour. Nazi power actually extended even beyond Europe: April 1941 saw the expulsion of the British from Libya at the hands of Rommel's Afrika Corps, May the capture of the strategic island of Crete in the eastern Mediterranean by German paratroopers, and at the same time, Rashid Ali, a pro-Nazi Arab nationalist, seized power in Iraq and requested German assistance.

Though welcoming this favourable Middle Eastern development, Hitler felt unable to assist it. His scale of military priorities was a rigid one. 'I have decided to encourage developments in the Middle East by supporting Iraq. Whether and by what means it may be possible . . . to oust the British from their position between the Mediterranean and the Persian Gulf cannot be decided until Operation Barbarossa is complete.'

Operation Barbarossa was the Nazi code-name for the attack on Russia, a military undertaking by far surpassing in scale and significance every other campaign of the 'greatest general of all times'. Already in *Mein Kampf* he had stated that 'Destiny itself seems to wish to point out the way to us there (i.e. to Russia). . . . This colossal Empire in the east is ripe for dissolution. . . .' In preparation for the imminent incorporation of this Empire into the Third Reich a whole complex of military, political and economic measures were being worked out during the spring of 1941. The following is an excerpt from a memorandum prepared by Goering's Economic Staff East, dealing with the future utilisation of material and human resources in Russia: 'Many tens of millions of people in the industrial areas will become redundant, and will either die or will have to emigrate to Siberia. Any attempt at saving the population there from death by starvation by importing surpluses . . . would reduce Germany's staying power. . . .'

To Hitler these were administrative details to be worked out by the appropriate departments inside the huge occupation apparatus he had set up. What concerned him were the grand, 'cosmic' concepts involved: Germany's destiny hinged on the possession of unlimited living space in the east—the breeding ground of the

YOU MAY HAVE BEGUN MAN – BUT I, ADOLF HITLER, WILL FINISH HIM

inferior Slav millions had to be conquered so that their numbers could be permanently kept down—Russia's defeat would sound the death knell of world Communism. He would be the world's saviour from the Red Peril—German occupation of Russia would make her the unchallenged master of the Eurasian land-mass—Britain would have to come to terms, followed by an America unable to hold her own against a vast German Reich with three times her population and allied to the great Asiatic Empire of Japan.

These were some of the grandiose ideas engaging Hitler's mind during the final preparations for what was to become the greatest and most devastating clash of armies in recorded history. It is no exaggeration to say that with Operation Barbarossa, Hitler was embarking on the greatest gamble of his unprecedented career: he would either make himself master of the entire globe, or in his unsuccessful bid, come close to destroying it.

10

Total War

HITLER, WHOSE SUPERSTITIOUS MIND often made him turn to astrology at decisive moments, launched his attack on Russia in the early dawn after the night of the midsummer solstice (22 June 1941). Afterwards he told his ministers: 'I shall never give up—even if it means war for a hundred years; there must never be a military power other than Germany west of the Urals.'

The pretext for Hitler's invasion of Russia, in so far as he felt any need for a pretext in a war launched without official declaration, was his claim that he was merely getting his blow in first to prevent an imminent Soviet attack on the Reich. There was no shred of truth in this. In fact, although Churchill had sent Stalin repeated warnings about German preparations for 'Operation Barbarossa', the Soviet dictator had unaccountably ignored them; thereby affording the rest of the world an unprecedented example either of political cynicism or political naïveté being carried to the degree of absurdity. Cynicism if he took Churchill's warning to be solely motivated by a selfish desire to embroil him in war with Hitler, and incredible naïveté if he believed even for a moment that to the Führer the Russo-German Non-Aggression Pact meant more than just another scrap of paper to be torn up at will.

The sudden Nazi assault along a 2,000-mile front found the Red Army quite unprepared—not merely on account of Stalin's blind self-delusion, but also because the recent series of purges had left the Soviet officer corps demoralised and woefully lacking in experienced commanders.

Consequently there was chaos in Russian frontier-districts which rapidly spread to the interior when Hitler unleashed his apparently irresistible combined force, a vast war machine consisting of 140 Wehrmacht divisions (19 of them armoured), 3 air fleets and large sections of the Italian, Hungarian, Rumanian, Finnish and Slovak armies. Backing up this offensive strength was the industrial might of the whole of continental Europe. As against this the Red Army depended for its supplies on an industrial system of very recent growth, a system which had furthermore been weakened by the purge of many of its best managers and technicians.

During the summer and autumn of 1941 the Wehrmacht over-ran huge areas with lightning speed and inflicted staggering losses in men and material on the Soviets. No previous invasion of Russia—not even Napoleon's or Ludendorff's—had opened with such successes. It seemed as if the incredibly ambitious targets of the Nazi offensive, Leningrad in the north, Moscow in the centre, and the food-producing Ukraine in the south, would be overrun according to plan.

Once again Hitler's own plan varied from that of his generals. There was disagreement among them about the relative priority to be given to each of the three main thrusts. Hitler decided to switch all available resources to the southern front, where huge encircling operations led to the capture of the whole Ukraine as far as the Don, and the destruction of Russian forces of over a million men.

Such triumphs were truly unprecedented and seemed to bear out Hitler's boast (in a speech in Berlin on 3 October 1941) that 'the enemy in the east has been struck down and will never rise again. Behind our troops there already lies a territory twice the size of the German Reich when I came to power in 1933.' But the priority the Führer had accorded to the Ukrainian campaign had meant a paring down of reserves for the central and northern thrusts, so that the Panzer spear-heads which approached the outskirts of Moscow and Leningrad in mid-autumn lacked the momentum required to over-run those major Soviet strongholds.

Soon the Russian winter set in with arctic severity. The 'greatest general of all times' was shown to have grossly miscalculated in his overweeningly arrogant assumption that the whole war in the east could be won in the short space of three months. He had fallen victim to his own propaganda about 'the vast Empire in the east being ripe for dissolution'.

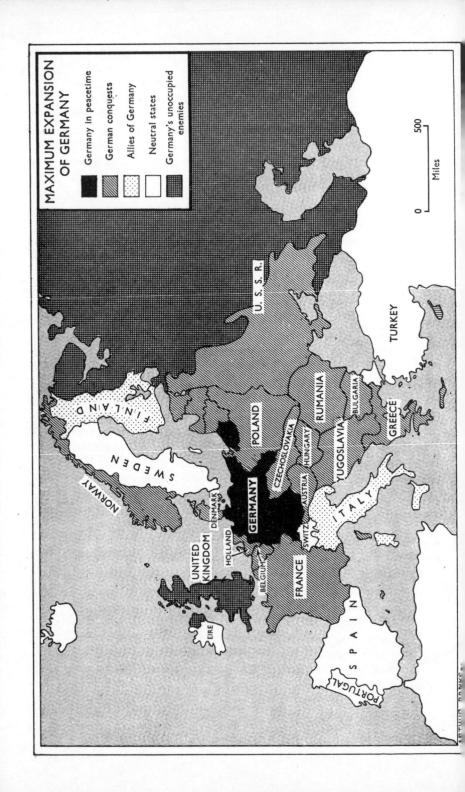

MAXIMUM EXPANSION
OF GERMANY

Germany in peacetime

German conquests

Allies of Germany

Neutral states

Germany's unoccupied
enemies

0   500

Miles

NORWAY

SWEDEN

FINLAND

U. S. S. R.

UNITED
KINGDOM

DENMARK

HOLLAND

EIRE

BELGIUM

GERMANY

POLAND

SWITZ.

CZECHOSLOVAKIA

AUSTRIA

HUNGARY

FRANCE

ITALY

YUGOSLAVIA

RUMANIA

BULGARIA

GREECE

TURKEY

SPAIN

PORTUGAL

The Wehrmacht found itself seriously unprepared for combat under Russian winter conditions, and frostbite accounted for German casualties on almost the same scale as the unexpected resilience of the Russian forces. The Red Army, whose losses in dead, wounded and captured ran into millions, had managed to escape annihilation in the huge pincer-movements of the Wehrmacht by trading space for time. In December they launched a counter-attack and scored their first purely local, but psychologically immensely important successes: the recapture of Rostov-on-Don from von Rundstedt's Southern Army group and the pushing back of von Kluge's Army from the immediate vicinity of Moscow.

On 7 December, Japan attacked the U.S. Pacific base of Pearl Harbour in a devastating air-raid—whilst her representatives in Washington were in the midst of negotiations with American officials. Hitler unhesitatingly followed the lead of his Asiatic anti-Comintern Pact partner and also declared war on the country of President Roosevelt, 'that creature of the Jews'.

World War II had thus reached truly global proportions, with six major powers locked in combat across the continents and oceans of the world. Germany, Italy and Japan, led by Hitler, Mussolini and Tojo were confronted by the countries of the Great Alliance under the leadership of the Big Three: Prime Minister Churchill, President Roosevelt and Marshal Stalin.

To Hitler events in the Pacific theatre of war were quite remote; the eastern front remained his major preoccupation both then and for the still remaining years of his rule. The Red Army's winter offensive had at first threatened to turn the Wehrmacht's retreat into a rout, but Hitler had intervened in matters of detailed military planning to good effect. Dismissing von Brauchitsch from his post as C.-in-C. of the army in the field, he had assumed command himself and stabilised the front line at great cost in manpower. It was his unshakable resolve that no German position, however untenable, should ever be abandoned to the Russians.

Having thus succeeded in holding the front, the Führer in the spring of 1942 decided to go over to a gigantic counter-attack involving strategic objectives in three continents. He ordered a huge two-pronged offensive to be mounted in southern Russia and North Africa, the aim of which was the eventual conquest of the whole area between the Red and Caspian Seas. In pursuing these vast objectives he was as yet quite undeterred by the steady build-up of Anglo-American air power, soon to be demonstrated by the first 1,000-bomber raid in history (Cologne, May 1942).

Rommel's Afrika Korps captured the important port of Tobruk and advanced to El Alamein, on the route to Alexandria, in accordance with the Führer-directive. The northern prong of what might have become the greatest pincer-movement in military annals, intended to inflict crippling blows not only on the Russians, but also on the British in the Middle East, was an immensely powerful thrust towards the oil-fields of the Caucasus and the bend of the Volga at Stalingrad.

This extension of the front towards the very threshold of Asia was beginning to impose a severe strain on the German war machine; the length of Wehrmacht communications both in Africa and Europe invited Allied counter-attacks. In Egypt and Libya these were at first aerial and naval, in Russia they consisted of large-scale partisan actions behind the German lines.

Towards the end of 1942 World War II was approaching its turning-point. The United States had been harnessing its enormous industrial and human potential to the war effort for almost a year; British forces in the Middle East were receiving decisive reinforcements from Australia and New Zealand. On 23 October 1942, Rommel's drive towards the Suez Canal was abruptly and disastrously terminated at El Alamein; Montgomery's Eighth Army broke through the German lines and commenced a 1000-mile pursuit of the 'Desert Fox' across the Libyan desert.

On 8 November, a joint Anglo-American force under General Eisenhower invaded French North Africa and thus threatened Rommel's base from the west. Hitler's immediate counter-measures included the complete annexation of hitherto unoccupied Vichy France and the despatch of troops to Tunisia.

In Russia the German offensive had reached the outskirts of Stalingrad, where the Volga makes an elbow-bend from its previous course to flow towards the Caspian Sea. The Sixth Army of General von Paulus was battering its way forward into the city with Russian soldiers and civilians contesting their advance street by street, house by house, inch by inch. Then on 19 November, three

Soviet army groups started counter-attacking north and south of Stalingrad; within five days this had led to the encirclement of twenty-two German divisions between the Volga and the Don.

Hitler's reaction to this grave threat was characteristic. He promoted General von Paulus to the rank of Field Marshal, to make him comply more readily with his own 'Supreme Commander's' directive to the surrounded soldiers: 'Stand and fight to the last man!'

General von Manstein in the meantime tried to relieve the Sixth Army by pushing a corridor through the encircling Russian divisions from his position further west, but this attack was thrown back. When von Paulus wanted to attempt a westward retreat so as to break out of the inexorably tightening Russian ring, the Führer ordered him peremptorily to abandon his plan. Germany's supreme war-lord unflinchingly maintained his resolve that not even one inch of ground was to be yielded by his soldiers in the east. He remained unmoved by the fate of 330,000 men of the Sixth Army, who in their commander's words 'were suffering unbearably through cold, hunger, epidemics and enemy action'.

Having endured these sufferings for almost three months, von Paulus surrendered to the Russians with the remnants of his decimated force on 31 January 1943. It was a historic turning-point for a number of reasons—one of them being that in all history no German Field Marshal had ever taken such a step. The Führer was aghast at von Paulus's lack of sacrificial courage. 'How can anyone be afraid of this moment of death? He could have ascended into eternity and national immortality. . . . The individual must die anyway.'

Yes, indeed, the individual had to die anyway. This much was true, but the individuals involved in Hitler's reckoning were to be counted not in ones or hundreds, not in thousands or hundred thousands; they literally numbered millions.

On 20 January 1942, a conference of Nazi leaders and government officials had taken place at Wannsee near Berlin. Prominent participants in these deliberations, which were interrupted by breaks for meals, included Adolf Eichmann and Reinhard Heydrich; the latter jocularly referred to the conference agenda as the 'Final Solution—with breakfast thrown in'.

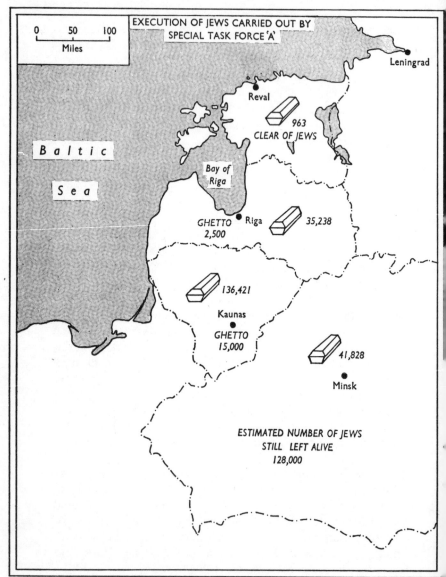

EXECUTION OF JEWS CARRIED OUT BY
SPECIAL TASK FORCE 'A'

0   50   100
Miles

Leningrad

Reval

963
CLEAR OF JEWS

B a l t i c

S e a

Bay of
Riga

GHETTO
2,500   Riga   35,238

136,421

Kaunas
GHETTO
15,000

41,828

Minsk

ESTIMATED NUMBER OF JEWS
STILL LEFT ALIVE
128,000

Redrawn from a top-secret SS document of 1942 dealing with the progress of genocide operations in eastern Europe

The conference protocol stated under the heading of Secret Reichs Matter:

'In the course of the final solution of the Jewish question, 11,000,000 Jews are involved. Under appropriate control these are to be employed in the east. . . . In large work-columns, the sexes strictly separated, the able-bodied Jews are to be used for road-building, in the course of which the majority will doubtless disappear through natural diminution.

'The possibly surviving remnant will have to be appropriately dealt with. . . .

'In the course of the final solution Europe is to be combed through from west to east. . . .

'The evacuated Jews will at first be conveyed in train-loads to transit ghettoes whence they will be further transported to the east . . . , etc.'

Thus was set in motion the deportation of all Jews from Nazi-occupied Europe to the ghettoes in Poland, from where they were to be sent further east 'to be appropriately dealt with'.

The 'appropriate treatment of the Jews' already in the east fell within the competence of four special task-forces (*Einsatzkommandos*) of the SS. Their naked victims were made to dig trenches, into which they were thrown after execution by shooting. This procedure was followed in all parts of Russia overrun by the Wehrmacht and involved nearly 2,000,000 Jews. The personnel of these Extermination Squads, consisting of SS men and police officials, was sometimes replenished by Wehrmacht volunteers, attracted to the unvarying routine of butchery by the promise of a threefold increase in pay, special leave and the prospect of loot.

When the Germans started retreating after the battle of Stalingrad early in 1943, a special detail of Jewish prisoners—Kommando 1005—was formed, whose task it was to re-open the mass-graves and to burn the half decayed corpses so as to wipe out all traces of the hideous massacres that had taken place. It was not until autumn 1944 that the Red Army, in the course of its great counter-offensive, reached an area in which they found Jews who were still alive.

But SS headquarters in Berlin, the so-called *Reichssicherheitshauptamt*, were dissatisfied with the crude and wasteful methods employed by the Einsatzkommandos. It was decided to substitute gassing for shooting. The extermination programme was to be organised in such a way that the greatest number of human beings could be wiped out with minimum effort in the shortest space of time. Special emphasis was placed on the economic utilisation of the by-products of extermination, such as gold teeth, hair, fat, etc.

Gigantic camps and ghettoes with populations comparable to those of major cities were set up, some of them attached to industrial plants in which the Jews performed slave-labour for such German industrial combines as I. G. Farben and Krupps. On arrival at these camps, of which Auschwitz was the largest, the Jews were 'selected', i.e. some were immediately gassed, while those who looked as though they could still be drained of the last ounce of their energy for the German war effort, were spared until such time as slave labour, disease and starvation, had rendered their continued existence superfluous. All elderly people, children and most women were automatically sent to the gas-chamber upon arrival.

Other camps, such as Treblinka, Maidanek and Sobibor were purely designed for extermination. They were literally industrial plants, producing death on the conveyor belt. At Treblinka each gas-chamber could accommodate 200 victims at one time. The substitution of Cyclon B for monoxide gas and the construction of gas-chambers for 2,000 people—technical improvements for which Auschwitz commandant Rudolf Hoess claimed the credit—appreciably reduced the time required for killing the victims and thereby helped to increase the 'turn-over' of Auschwitz, that greatest death-factory of all time.

Referring to his innovations Hoess stated at his war-crimes trial:

'It now only took from three to fifteen minutes to kill the people in chambers, according to climatic conditions. We knew when the people were dead because their screaming stopped. . . . After the bodies were removed our special commandos (i.e. special squads of Jewish inmates), took off the rings and extracted the gold from the teeth of the corpses.'

The special commandos then removed the gassed corpses to giant crematoria for burning; the ashes were scattered over the

Polish countryside or, as in the case of Auschwitz, dumped into the waters of the near-by Vistula.

By the summer of 1944 Eichmann was able to report to Himmler that approximately 4,000,000 Jews had been killed in the various camps, in addition to which a further 2,000,000 had been liquidated by the Einsatzkommandos in Russia. The main executors of Hitler's verbal order for the Final Solution, apart from Himmler and Eichmann, were SS Generals Müller and Reinhard Heydrich.

Heydrich was the first of the 'genocide experts' to share the fate of his numberless victims. He was assassinated in May 1942 by members of the Czech resistance. The SS claimed that the trail of his 'murderers' led to the mining village of Lidice. As an object lesson to all would-be resisters, the population of Lidice was massacred, and the village razed to the ground.

But the resistance movements of Occupied Europe were not intimidated. When the Germans annexed Vichy France outright after the Allied landings in North Africa, the French sailors at Toulon scuttled their ships to prevent them falling into enemy hands. In Yugoslavia partisan warfare commenced in 1942 and continued in spite of mass execution of hostages. In the middle of the war there were already mountain areas in Serbia where Hitler's writ did not run. In Amsterdam the railway workers struck in protest against the first deportations of Jews to Auschwitz, but their resistance was smashed by arrests and executions, and the untimetabled railway service, with its overcrowded outward and ominously empty return trains, was soon resumed.

Having written off the Sixth Army, Hitler once again managed to effect a temporary stabilisation of his now rather shorter eastern front early in 1943. The Wehrmacht extricated its advanced units from the Caucasus sector and deployed them in the Ukraine and Crimea. In March they recaptured Kiev; it seemed as if the previous year's pattern of Russian winter advances and summer retreats was about to be repeated. But the over-all balance of power was slowly and inexorably changing to Hitler's detriment.

Rommel, Germany's most popular soldier, was driven out of North Africa as the result of attacks by the British from the east, Americans from the west and Free French from the south. He was forced to abandon a quarter of a million German and Italian soldiers who were taken prisoner by the Allies.

The Mediterranean was thereby re-opened to Allied shipping; Malta, which had withstood ceaseless Luftwaffe bombardment, was allowed to breathe again. The Russians who had at last managed to loosen the Wehrmacht's noose around Moscow were insistently demanding that their Western Allies open a 'Second Front', i.e. launch an invasion in western Europe and impose a two-front war on an already retreating enemy.

The Western Allies took note of Russia's request and invaded Europe (June 1943), but not in the direction indicated by Stalin. Anglo-Amercian assault troops landed in Sicily as a stepping-stone towards Italy, which Churchill, with greater political than geographical justifications had described as, the 'soft under-belly of Axis Europe'. (Earlier unsuccessful Allied commando raids on Dieppe and St Nazaire had convinced Western leaders that Nazi defences along the French coast could only be breached at prohibitive cost in men and materials.)

Under the impact of the Allied landings in Sicily the Italian King responded to a patriotic initiative of the Grand Council of the Fascist party and dismissed Mussolini from the leadership of the country. The ex-Duce was arrested on the orders of his successor, Marshal Badoglio. A little later, shortly after the September landings of Anglo-American forces in southern Italy, the Badoglio government took Italy out of the Axis Alliance, and the war, by signing a separate armistice with the Allies.

Hitler reacted speedily and decisively. German units in Italy occupied Rome and disarmed the Italian army. Mussolini was rescued from Badoglio's prison in a daring raid led by SS Colonel Skorzeny and flown north, where he was pressed by Hitler into acting as the figure-head of a new Fascist government under German auspices. The resuscitated Duce meted out savage punishment to all Fascist officials who had turned against him at the time of his deposition. He had Ciano (his ex-Foreign Minister and son-in-law) executed by a firing squad, and threw himself whole-heartedly into the task of forming new dependable Italian axis divisions, the so-called Fascist Militia, soon to be engaged in heavy fighting with pro-Allied and Communist Italian partisans in the northern mountains and plains.

In the meantime the Anglo-American advance up the Italian peninsula was proceeding slowly but relentlessly. Naples was liberated in October 1943 and Rome not before June 1944—the Germans under their commander, Field Marshal Kesselring, contesting every step of the way.

Stalin felt that the Allies had proved by their failure to invade western Europe that they intended Russia to carry the main burden of the war, and considered the Italian campaign an inadequate substitute for the Second Front. But on the other hand the Russians had every reason to be grateful for the badly-needed supplies from Allied sources which were reaching their front in ever-increasing volume, either via the overland route through Persia, or by the sea-route from Britain to Murmansk, past lethal Nazi U-boat lairs in Norwegian fjords by which Hitler set great store.

Submarine warfare had become central to Hitler's design for knocking Britain out of the war by denying her the overseas supplies without which she could be reduced to starvation within a few weeks. Whilst at the beginning of 1941 there were only six Nazi U-boats operating along Allied shipping routes at any one time, this figure had increased ten-fold by the end of that year. In 1942 Allied losses due to the Nazi submarine campaign had risen to 900 vessels totalling 6,250,000 gross tons. This success was so gratifying that shipbuilding workers employed in German U-boat yards were henceforth exempted from military service, which in turn led to the construction of over 300 new U-boats the following year. In January 1943 the U-boat chief Doenitz replaced Admiral Raeder as head of the German navy. His promotion underlined the importance which Hitler now attached to the developing U-boat offensive in north-western waters. But these decisions were taken too late to affect the course of the war decisively. At this critical stage, Germany's resources were irretrievably over-committed in the east.

In July 1943 the Red Army was in a position to launch its first summer offensive. It wiped out the Wehrmacht's Kursk salient and proceeded throughout the autumn to re-capture such vital positions as Smolensk, Kharkov and Kiev.

January 1944 finally saw the lifting of the threat to Leningrad, which had been practically cut off by the Germans for endless months. Russian units on that front were beginning to push forward into the Baltic states, whilst Red Army spearheads 2,000 miles further south were simultaneously approaching the Rumanian frontier. Yet despite all these reverses, the German withdrawal, or 'shortening of the front line', to use the phrase invariably employed in Nazi communiqués, proceeded smoothly and the Wehrmacht still disposed of sufficient reserves in morale and manpower to launch counter-attacks capable of slowing down the Russian advance.

This great defensive effort owed a lot to Hitler himself, who from the remoteness of his headquarters in the East Prussian forests issued a stream of 'Führer-directives' by which he regulated every sphere of the war effort. Most of his generals knew full well by this time that the war could not possibly be won, but Hitler maintained the inflexible conviction that victory would yet be his.

'The time will come when the tension between the Allies (i.e. the Anglo-Americans on one side and the Russians on the other) will become so great that the break will occur. All the coalitions throughout history have disintegrated sooner or later. The only thing is to wait for the right moment, no matter how hard it is. Since the year 1941 it has been my task not to lose my nerve, under any circumstances; instead whenever there is a collapse, my task has been to find a way out and a remedy in order to restore the situation.'

Time after time military and civilian experts who had come to see Hitler in the full knowledge that the war was as good as lost, left his presence carried along, against their better judgement, by his fanatical belief in the *Endsieg* (final victory). And so the generals and the administrators and the technicians continued to perform their allotted tasks with patriotic dedication and high professional skill, as indeed did the German people as a whole. As Himmler told SS commanders: 'Our workers are on the whole so filled with a sense of the faithful execution of their obligations in this war that they create no difficulties for us.' What was it that made 75,000,000 people prosecute a war effort that daily stood less chance of succeeding? Were they still dedicated to the vision of the Nazi millennium, the thousand-year Reich, which Churchill had characterised as 'a new Dark Age made more sinister and perhaps more protracted by the lights of perverted science'; an Empire which was to have only one *raison d'être*: to perpetuate itself for the sake of German national glory?

Or were they genuinely afraid that an Allied victory would, as Goebbels threatened day in day out, expose Germany to the atrocities of Stalin's 'Mongolian hordes' and the vindictiveness of 'Roosevelt and his Jewish wire-pullers' such as Henry Morgenthau? (The latter, a member of the US cabinet, had mooted a post-war project under which Germany was to be deprived of all industry, and would therefore revert to a pastoral mode of existence.)

Were there not in 1944 some Germans who felt that things could not be allowed to continue as they had done for over a decade? Such earlier anti-Nazi resistance as there had been after 1933 had soon died out, partly on account of the Gestapo terror, but largely because the German public increasingly identified itself with the actions and ideals of the Hitler regime. There had been outstanding individuals—such as the Pacifist Nobel Laureate, Carl von Ossietzky and the Evangelical Pastor Niemöller—prepared to speak out at the risk of death or concentration camp imprisonment, but it had seemed as if theirs were voices crying in the wilderness.

During the closing stages of the war, some sort of shocked realisation of the horrifying scale of Nazi atrocities must have come to a great number of Germans. Many members of the Wehrmacht witnessed, if they did not participate in, massacres of Jews and executions of hostages and captured partisans; others must have had personal experience of conditions obtaining in the inhumanly overcrowded Stalags for Russian prisoners of war, where unbearable pangs of hunger reduced many inmates to the level of cannibalism. When these prisoners were moved from one camp to another or to slave-labour projects, guards could often be dispensed with, because huge columns of emaciated Russians would apathetically trudge behind the mobile soup-kitchen leading the procession. Or had the Germans who had witnessed these scenes of human degradation only seen in them further confirmation of Nazi teachings on the sub-human character of the Slav races?

There were indeed a few Germans prepared to listen to the voice of their conscience and to help the pitiful victims of their own fellow countrymen; they thereby often only forfeited their own lives in addition to those of the people they tried to save.

It was not from among them that effective resistance to Hitler could come, for they were too few, too impotent to accomplish anything except individual acts of mercy. There was only one group inside the Third Reich still capable of independent action: the army. And it was indeed among the officer corps that the most effective schemes against Hitler, such as they were, were conceived. Chief of General Staff von Beck, who had resigned before Munich, had at various times managed to engage the tentative interest of commanders as highly placed as von Brauchitsch, Halder and Rommel. Nothing had come of this for reasons outlined in an earlier chapter. But now, with Germany heading for defeat, Beck's views found wider acceptance in army circles, and something like the nucleus of a military resistance was coming into being.

In 1943 General von Tresckow and his adjutant von Schla-brendorff had placed a time-tomb in the Führer's plane on its flight back from the Russian front. It had failed to explode and von Schlabrendorff had had the presence of mind immediately to fly back to Hitler's HQ, where he dismantled the bomb before it could be discovered.

Vaguely co-ordinating their efforts with this military resistance were a number of anti-Nazi politicians who had survived from the Weimar era. Chief among them was the ex-Lord Mayor of Leipzig, Dr Goerdeler, who with others had been working out plans for Germany's post-Hitler government and constitution. These circles had tried to contact Allied representatives in neutral countries to obtain assurances of support for themselves in case they managed to take power, but Allied policy, ever since the Teheran Conference of the Big Three in 1943, had been firmly based on the idea of Germany's unconditional surrender as the only possible ending for the war.

At Teheran, Churchill, Roosevelt and Stalin had also concerted the final measures designed to smash Nazi Germany. The enemy was to be attacked from three directions: through Poland, which the Red Army reached in the winter of 1943-44, through Italy, still the scene of German holding operations and, most important of all, through France where the Western Allies intended to open the long-awaited Second Front some time in 1944.

Yet Hitler was not to be caught unprepared. A huge system of coastal defence fortifications was established in the invasion areas of France and Belgium—work which was carried out by a vast slave-labour force under the direction of the pitilessly efficient supreme Nazi task-masters, Sauckel and Todt. (At the end of the war there were nearly 5,000,000 foreign workers in Germany. This figure had been boosted to almost 7,000,000 by conscripting the labour of prisoners of war and concentration camp inmates.)

Mindful of the old adage about attack being the best form of defence, Hitler at the same time accorded top priority to the development of the *Vergeltungs Waffen* (revenge weapons), the long-awaited 'secret weapons' which were yet to give Germany final victory. The V-weapons became a recurring theme of Nazi propaganda, and were presented to the millions of town-dwellers exposed to heavy Allied air-attacks as an advance guarantee that their sufferings at the hands of the RAF would soon be repaid with interest.

The first of these secret weapons, the V-1 or 'doodle-bug', was launched against London on 13 June 1944, but its effect was completely over-shadowed by the fact that the Second Front had been opened a week earlier. The massive sea-borne Anglo-American invasion of Normandy which, commencing on 6 June (D-Day), gathered ever-greater momentum under the protective umbrella of overwhelming Allied air power, made Germany's defeat a foregone conclusion. The anti-Hitler opposition now felt that the rapidly deteriorating situation made swift action imperative.

The initiative as far as inner German resistance was concerned, now passed into the hands of Colonel von Stauffenberg, who was serving at Reserve Army HQ, Berlin, after having been severely wounded in North Africa. He had been picked to attend a conference at Hitler's headquarters on 20 July to present a report. On that crucial occasion his briefcase contained, besides the plans due to be presented, a bomb with a timing device. Having previously set the detonating mechanism, he placed his briefcase under the table, on which were spread large maps that Hitler was studying in the company of General Keitel. Stauffenberg then left the room on a pretext and within a minute an explosion took place.

Managing to get past the check-point by a ruse, Stauffenberg flew back to Berlin, convinced that Hitler was dead. He informed von Beck and his fellow-conspirators who were waiting at the General Staff building of this, and they in turn sent out messages to army commanders all over Occupied Europe, instructing them to pledge their allegiance to the new government and to disarm all SS formations in their command area.

But most of the army leaders obeyed the counter-directives Keitel had in the meantime issued from Hitler's HQ, informing them that the Führer was still alive, though slightly injured and suffering from shock, and they paid no heed to Beck's message. The only notable exception was General Stülpnagel in Paris, whose Wehrmacht units surrounded the local SS barracks, disarmed the black-uniformed scourges of the French capital, and put them in custody.

Yet by this time the conspirators in Berlin had already been taken prisoner by troops loyal to the Führer and summarily sentenced to death by court-martial. Whilst von Beck was granted the special privilege of putting an end to his own life, Stauffenberg and the others faced a firing squad. Stauffenberg died crying: 'Long Live Free Germany!'

The cry found no echo. Free Germany remained unborn, it required the midwife of total defeat; as yet Hitler lived on. He proved it tangibly by broadcasting over the national network shortly after midnight of 20 July.

'If I speak to you today, it is first in order that you should hear my voice and should know that I am unhurt, and secondly that you should know of a crime unparalleled in German history. . . . The bomb exploded two metres to my right. . . . I myself only sustained scratches, bruises and burns. I regard this as a confirmation of the task imposed upon me by Providence. . . . I am convinced that with the uncovering of this tiny clique of traitors, there has at long last been created in the rear that atmosphere which the fighting front needs. This time we shall get even with them in the way to which we National Socialists are accustomed.'

This customary way was indicated by death sentences on 4,890 persons connected with the 'tiny clique of traitors'. Field Marshal von Witzleben, along with some other generals, was executed by slow hanging from meat-hooks; a film of this bestial procedure was later screened in the Führer's private cinema. Many disappeared into concentration camps; some forestalled this fate by taking their own lives, among them Field Marshal Rommel. He had actually been unconscious in hospital on the crucial day (as the result of a British air-raid), but Gestapo enquiries had revealed previous treasonable contact with von Beck. When he had sufficiently recovered from his air-raid injuries, a Führer message offered him the alternative of a treason trial or suicide. He chose suicide for his family's sake. The official communiqué ascribed his death to heart failure; Field Marshal von Rundstedt's final words at the state funeral were 'Rommel's heart had belonged to the Führer'.

In the absence of any other military leader prepared to take action against Hitler, there was now no hope of the war ending before the last act had been played out to the full. Germany's soldiers and civilians appeared quite resigned to carry on to the bitter end; either until the Final Victory of Hitler's obsessed vision, or until the promise of the Nazi marching song, 'The Universe shall lie in ruins, when German warriors meet their doom', had been fulfilled literally.

11

The Last Act

WARSAW HAD BEEN Europe's first capital to endure the horrors of aerial bombardment in World War II. Now in the summer of 1944, it became a battlefield once again. The Russians had resumed their advance shortly after the Allied invasion of Normandy and had recaptured Minsk and Vilna, destroying half the Wehrmacht divisions facing them on the central front in the process. The Polish Home Army judged the moment opportune to stage a rising in Warsaw with the intention of liberating the capital from Nazi rule before its occupation by the Red Army and consequent absorption in the Russian sphere of influence. This rising was marked by feats of unimaginable Polish heroism, but was eventually crushed after sixty-three days—a desperate stand doomed to failure by the lack of indispensable outside support.

The Red Army's advance had in the meantime been halted by German counter-attacks—but by flatly denying the RAF refuelling facilities the Russians were also making it impossible for the Western Allies to assist the Poles. The Warsaw insurgents were gradually reduced by the SS division *Dirlewanger*, which was in the main recruited from released German criminals. The remorseless destruction of the Polish capital by heavy artillery and flame-throwers was accompanied by an orgy of pillage and torture. None of this weighed sufficiently with the Russians to make them come to the aid of the Polish Home Army; a dreadful example of history repeating itself, for fifteen months earlier the Home Army had done very little to sustain the Warsaw Ghetto Fighters in their forlorn last stand to prevent the deportation of all Jews to the death camps. The entire ghetto area had been razed to the ground—this process of destruction continued throughout the Warsaw Rising of 1944. When the Russians finally pushed the Germans out by the spring of 1945, only ten per cent of the capital's buildings were still inhabitable, the rest was a gigantic mass of rubble.

Early in September 1944, with the Allies in occupation of large parts of northern France, the Germans launched their first V-2. This rocket-type 'revenge weapon' could inflict heavy civilian casualties—a direct hit on an east London block of flats caused hundreds of deaths—but the Allied advance towards the V-2 launching sites along the Channel coast eventually put paid to this last hope of Hitler's for staving off defeat.

Shortly after the first V-2 raid on London, American advanced columns crossed the German frontier near Aachen. The British, who had raced eastwards to the north of this American thrust, liberated Brussels and then attempted to turn the German flank by dropping airborne forces at Arnhem in Holland.

But this operation turned out to be a costly failure; Germany proved herself to be still possessed of considerable reserves of strength. It was in order to utilise the last reserves of his man-power that Hitler had created a new fighting force of hurriedly-trained civilians—the *Volkssturm*—into which all able-bodied males between 16 and 60 were compulsorily drafted. In fact the fighting potential of which Hitler could dispose of at this late stage of the war still amounted to about 10,000,000 men, three-quarters of them in the formations of the Wehrmacht or SS. The effectiveness of this force was, however, reduced quite considerably by Hitler's obdurateness in keeping it dispersed over half Europe.

Units which might have materially assisted in the defence of Germany were on the Führer's insistence kept guarding submarine bases in Norway, rocket-launching sites in Holland, U-boat training grounds along the Baltic and bauxite quarries in Hungary.

But there was also a credit side to this account. The jealously guarded bauxite supplies from Hungary enabled the German air-craft industry to turn out nearly three times as many fighters by September 1944 as it had done in January. Under the overall direction of the ex-architect Albert Speer, many other branches of Germany's war industry registered comparable increases in output. In this last autumn of the war, this impressive production record was only contradicted in two major spheres: tank production was declining and oil reserves were approaching exhaustion. This may well have been due to the incessant Allied air attacks which were quite often carried out by 1,000 bombers at a time.

The last major German counter-attack was launched during the winter. It was intended to reach the Belgian coast and to recapture the important Allied supply base of Antwerp. Hitler committed some of General Rundstedt's last intact divisions to this surprise thrust against the Americans manning the Ardennes sector of the front. He managed to halt the Allied advance temporarily, but after a few days of very heavy fighting, the bulge in the front had been straightened out again, at a cost of 120,000 German, as compared with 70,000 American casualties.

The Russians, acting in conjunction with Tito's partisan armies, had driven the Wehrmacht out of Belgrade in October 1944, after which they pushed northwards up the Danube Valley and stormed Budapest early in 1945. At the Yalta Conference (February 1945), Churchill, Roosevelt and Stalin made dispositions concerning the future of liberated Europe and once again affirmed their determination to continue the war until Germany's unconditional surrender. British forces were by this time advancing towards the Lombardy plain and liberating Greece, where their restoration of the monarchy provoked violent Communist reactions.

In March the Americans crossed the Rhine and carried the war into parts of Germany which had remained unscathed by its effects since the days of Napoleon. Russian forces, 3,000,000 strong and thirsting for revenge, were at the same time advancing into eastern Germany on a broad front which stretched from the Baltic to Silesia. They had witnessed the dreadful evidence of what Hitler's New Order had meant to the peoples of eastern Europe and were determined to settle scores with its perpetrators. Their advance was preceded by the westward movement of huge columns of German refugees, panic-stricken lest 'the hordes of Stalin's asiatic barbarians' inflict pillage and rape upon them.

After the failure of the Ardennes offensive, Hitler had not returned to his East Prussian forest HQ. He had allowed himself to be persuaded by Goebbels, whose fanatical devotion to Nazism was in no way affected by the ever-increasing probability of defeat, to stay on in Berlin. Goebbels felt that Hitler's place in the final phase of the struggle was among his own people. The

Führer who had increasingly isolated himself from his loyal subjects as the war progressed (he had, for instance, never visited bombed towns to comfort air-raid victims), acted on Goebbels' advice, but in a significantly different manner. He simply went to earth in the Reich Chancellery's bomb- and noise-proof shelter. From this subterranean bunker he continued to direct the defence of his rapidly shrinking empire. From here he ordered army groups which no longer existed outside his deluded mind to counter-attack along fronts long since overrun by the Allies. In this underground hide-out, daylight and reality alike were completely shut out, and the Führer's brain was turning towards the destruction, not only of his opponents, but also of those who had for so long loyally supported him—the German people.

When Armaments Minister Albert Speer wrote to him pleading for measures to be taken that would at least safeguard the subsistence level of the population, 'since the end of the war could only bring defeat and chaos', he received the following reply:

'If the war is to be lost the nation will also perish. There is no need to consider the basis of the most primitive existence any longer. On the contrary it is better to destroy even that and to destroy it ourselves. The nation has proved itself weak and the future belongs solely to the stronger eastern nations. Besides those who remain after the battle are of little value—for the good have fallen.'

Vienna, Greater Germany's second city, fell to the Russians on 13 April 1945. But in Hitler's drug-sedated mind this reverse was totally over-shadowed by a news item received from America a little earlier behind which he claimed to be able to detect the hand of Providence.

On the previous day, United States President F. D. Roosevelt, whom his countrymen had three times re-elected to what had by now become the most important and onerous office in the world, had finally succumbed to the combined pressure of prolonged ill-health and thirteen years' strenuous over-work. Hitler's clouded brain seized on this fortuitous event as an omen presaging a miraculous change for the better in Germany's fortunes, just as nearly two centuries earlier Prussia had been saved from imminent defeat at the hands of a European coalition by the sudden death of the Russian Tsarina Elizabeth. (The new Tsar, Peter III, had dropped out of the anti-Prussian alliance and had concluded a separate peace with Frederick the Great.)

Since Roosevelt was known to have acted as a badly-needed conciliator between Churchill and Stalin at the Big Three meetings, Hitler assumed that his removal from the scene would result in the divergence of interest between the Soviets and the Western democracies, already exemplified by mutual recriminations over Poland and Greece, becoming sufficiently acute to disrupt the whole Allied coalition. On 16 April the Führer issued an Order of the Day in which Roosevelt's death was accorded Providential significance:

> 'From this moment when fate has taken the greatest war criminal of all times from this earth the war will take a decisive turn' (i.e. a turn for the better as far as the Reich's fortunes were concerned).

This illusion was speedily shattered. On 25 April, American and Russian spearheads linked up at Torgau on the Elbe amidst scenes of genuine fraternisation. The Reich was now cut in half. Goering and other Nazi leaders had already left Berlin, which was coming under Russian shell-fire, for the Alpine region of Bavaria. It was in the Alps that Hitler had fleetingly planned to establish a southern redoubt, a mountain-girt stronghold which was to be well-nigh impregnable.

But Hitler now resolved not to leave the Reich capital under any circumstances short of death. His closest and most loyal companion in embattled Berlin was Goebbels, who made his own wife and numerous children share the Führer's mole-like existence in the Bunker. Goering telegraphed from the comparative safety of Bavaria, asking to be officially proclaimed the Führer's successor in the event of Hitler's death, whilst in the north SS Chief Himmler, who had prepared the ground by previously stopping the organised killing of Jews in the camps, had begun separate peace negotiations with the Western Allies through Count Bernadotte of Sweden.

The news of the treachery of Goering and Himmler, both of them until recently among his closest associates, threw Hitler into convulsions of rage. He stripped them of all State and Party positions and appointed loyal underlings in their stead. Then, at last realising the war was irrevocably lost, he turned his attention to such matters as his marriage and the drawing up of his political testament. In the streets of Berlin outside the concrete-protected isolation of the Chancellery all was confusion and death. Military police were hanging Wehrmacht deserters from the lamp-posts. Fourteen-year-old Hitler Youths tried to bar the advance of Russian tanks with hand grenades and died with the Führer's name on their lips. When Red Army units approached dangerously close to the Chancellery, Hitler ordered sections of the Berlin Underground to be flooded to delay their advance and hundreds of Berliners, sheltering from air-raids, were engulfed by the surging tide.

Early in the morning of 29 April, Hitler married Eva Braun at a civil ceremony in the Bunker. She was an ex-employee of his personal photographer Hoffmann, and had been the Führer's secret mistress for years. A few hours later news reached them that Mussolini and his mistress Clara Petacci had been captured and shot by Italian partisans and their corpses hung upside down in a Milan square to be spat on by the crowd. Hitler made no comment on hearing the macabre account of the end of his erstwhile mentor and subsequent junior partner; at this stage, his message to posterity, the 'Political Testament', probably occupied his mind to the exclusion of everything else.

'More than 30 years have now passed, since I in 1914 made my modest contribution as a volunteer in the First World War which was forced upon the Reich. . . . It is untrue that I or anyone else in Germany wanted war in 1939. It was desired and instigated by those international statesmen who were either of Jewish descent or worked for Jewish interests. . . . I have never wished that after the fatal First World War a Second against England or even America should break out. Centuries will pass away, but out of the ruins of our towns and monuments the hatred against those finally responsible will grow; that race, Jewry, which is the real culprit of this murderous struggle. I die with a happy heart. . . . From the sacrifice of our soldiers and my own unity with them unto death will in any case spring up in the history of Germany the seed of a valiant renaissance of the National Socialist movement and thus of the realisation of a true community of nations.'

185

The testament continued with Hitler's dispositions for the future government of the Reich. He designated Grand Admiral von Doenitz (of U-boat fame) as his successor to be assisted by Goebbels and Party boss Bormann. The testament concluded by enjoining upon the new governing triumvirate and the whole German nation 'scrupulous observance of the racial laws and unmerciful resistance to the universal poisoner of all nations, international Jewry'.

The wheel had come full circle; Nazism ended as it had begun: in deathly hate.

Next morning, 30 April, Hitler assembled the Chancellery staff and said farewell. The Russians were now only a few streets away. When Hitler announced his decision to commit suicide, some of the Chancellery personnel could hardly conceal their sense of relief. A raucous celebration got under way in the soldiers' canteen; the noise grew so loud that a message came from Hitler's quarters ordering silence. At 3 p.m., having again said goodbye to Goebbels and Bormann—Doenitz was away at Naval HQ at Flensburg—Hitler shot himself through the mouth. His body and that of Eva Braun, who had taken poison, were carried out into the courtyard of the Chancellery, soaked in petrol and burnt.

Goebbels and Bormann made a last desperate attempt at negotiating with the Russian commander, General Zhukov. His only reply was a demand for unconditional surrender. Consequently Goebbels followed his Führer's example on the following day. He gave poison to his wife and six children—a world without Hitler was not fit to live in. Then he ordered an SS man to shoot him. Their bodies were burnt. As to Bormann's movements at that time and afterwards, nothing definite is known.

Doenitz announced his own succession over the radio and spoke of Hitler dying as a hero in the capital of the Reich. He appealed to the German people to continue the struggle against Bolshevism, still hoping, at this late hour, to divide the Allies. His term of office lasted five days. On 7 May, General Jodl, on behalf of the command of the Wehrmacht, signed the unconditional surrender of all German forces at Rheims in the presence of American, British, French and Russian representatives.

The Third Reich had ceased to exist. Estimates of the number of human lives lost as the result of its existence vary between

35,000,000 and 40,000,000; that is, not very much less than the total population of all the counties of England. The material losses sustained by an entire continent were astronomical, the moral damage incalculable.

Not a year has passed since World War II when there has not been a War Crimes trial for the purpose of meting out retribution to the men who had loosed upon Europe a system harnessing the resources of technical civilisation to the impulses of barbarism, a system sterile of any innovation conceivably beneficial to man, whose legacy has still not been entirely liquidated.

The Third Reich

NO PERIOD in German history poses more perplexing problems than the Nazi era. Since 1945 one question above all has kept recurring in the minds of people everywhere, 'How was it possible for a civilised country like Germany to relapse into a state of barbarism without precedent in the annals of man?'

This is a question we cannot hope to answer exhaustively since it would involve probing into such disparate fields of study as social psychology, education, culture, economics, politics and religion. Yet an attempt, however cursory, at answering it must be made.

We have seen how historical circumstances had prevented a genuine democratic tradition from taking root in Germany. By an unfortunate concatenation of events democracy had been made to appear to many Germans as synonymous with internal and external weakness. Hitler had, on the other hand, from the very inception of his reign gone from strength to strength, producing a veritable chain-reaction of successes in which all Germans could share emotionally, and quite a few materially. Long before foreign conquest had vastly increased the scope of Nazi patronage, the purge of non-Nazis and Jews from all positions in public life and the establishment of a party apparatus, almost duplicating the existing civil service, had created a large vested interest of new office-holders deeply indebted to the regime.

Even if prior to 1939 there were still isolated stirrings of non-conformity inside Germany, the advent of war added the pressures of patriotism and apparent invincibility to the already existing ones of propaganda and terror to weld almost all the 80,000,000 inhabitants of the Greater Reich into a uniform mass. Opposition to the regime at such time could at best be a futile gesture, at worst a suicidal undertaking unlikely to achieve anything. When the tide of battle was turning against them, the attitude of most Germans was still one of 'my country right or wrong!' Even in the concluding stages of the war there was an all-pervasive mood of 'seeing it through to the bitter end'—a resolve to which collective fear of Allied retribution in no small measure contributed.

The phrase 'whether for good or ill, Hitler is our destiny', sums up the feeling of dependence on their leadership which the overwhelming majority retained right up to the collapse. Our investigation will therefore centre upon this feeling of dependence, the circumstances under which it arose and the methods whereby the regime perpetuated it.

Its roots lay in the situation of permanent crisis after 1918 when to so many Germans all the old values and certainties had crumbled into nothingness and the problem of arriving at correct decisions in a perplexing world seemed insuperable. This situation had ended with the arrival of a charismatic leader offering to relieve the Germans of the burden of having to work out their own destinies. In addition to allaying their 'fear of freedom' by taking all decision-making into his own hands, Hitler also reassured the dependent millions by the rightness (i.e. success) of his decisions.

This great dependence of the Germans also stemmed from the fact that so very few among them had a positive political faith with which to oppose the activist dynamic of Nazism. Liberalism was tainted with ineffectuality and failure, democratic conservatism an unknown concept and social democracy anathema to the middle classes. Such among the workers as still upheld their former beliefs frequently dissipated their energies in Socialist-Communist recrimination.

Another possible factor militating against total Nazi control of the Germans' minds might have been the religious attachments evinced by millions of members enrolled in the Protestant and Catholic Churches. Yet, whilst due cognisance should be taken of religious resistance, exemplified by various Catholic prelates as well as Pastor Niemöller and others of the Protestant Confessional Church who refused to bow down to Baal, the general attitude of both clergy and laity was based on the time-honoured precept: render unto Caesar the things that are Caesar's. The quietist, purely spiritual aspect of German religiosity also made possible the co-existence within one and the same social group (i.e. the middle class), of a large church membership and of a very significant body of opinion inspired by Nietzsche's anti-religious philosophy. Nietzsche's ideas held such an attraction for the educated German public that during the Great War every soldier was allegedly carrying a copy of *Thus Spake Zarathustra* in his knapsack. 'God is dead' was the assumption that served as a starting point of Nietzsche's philosophy. That the path to human advancement in a Godless universe could only be discerned by a few rare individuals, so-called supermen, was its conclusion. To inaugurate the reign of the superman, the world would have to be cleansed of the slave-morality of Christianity, as well as of the enfeebling egalitarian creeds of Liberalism and Socialism, since the continued sway of such concepts as charity and brotherly love would drag the supermen down to the level of the undifferentiated mass. Christianity was 'the one great curse, the one enormous and innermost perversion . . . the one immortal blemish of mankind'.

Nietzsche's corrosive effect on religious and moral thinking was still further intensified by the popularisation and corruption of the ideas of Darwin; terms like 'the survival of the fittest', 'the struggle for existence', etc., were used by politicians, professors and cranks, long before Hitler wrote *Mein Kampf* to point the lesson that the laws of life were those of conflict and that notions of pity and tolerance were snares the weak had devised for the strong.

The final erosion of all moral values was effected by the propagation of the doctrine of racism, a doctrine elevated into an all-embracing philosophy by the Nazis. The spurious philosophy of race was inflated until it had a bearing on every facet of human existence, whether it be history, law, language, or even science. (Einsteinian physics, for instance, were impugned as typically Jewish, i.e. too preoccupied with numerical calculations.) Racism was the culmination of the whole process by which the Germans were—partly actively, partly passively—transformed from human beings into scientific barbarians.

This new barbarism was scientific not only in the sense of having the resources of modern technology at its disposal, but also on account of being buttressed by 'scientific' statements such as the following, taken in the main from the writings of academic experts on race during the Nazi era:

'The Nordic race pioneered all religions, since the solar myths which were the earliest forms of religion could only originate among people to whom the sun was a cosmic experience.'

'History is determined not by the conflict of ideas or classes, but of races; for example, the French Revolution was the revenge taken by the Celtic element on the Germanic one in French eighteenth-century society.'

'The Jews exude an inherent repulsive odour (the *foetor Judaicus*) which in the Middle Ages was wrongly believed to be removable by baptismal water.'

'The close resemblance of such word-pairs as God and Goth, or Slav and slave is no mere accident; it is an expression of folk-wisdom deeply rooted in language.'

'Jewish influence is so corrupting that a person reading a book by a Jewish author will adopt a crooked stance without even being aware of it.'

'The Germanic hosts who smashed the Mediterranean Empire had the right to act in this way conferred upon them by their own boundless strength. To censure them for it would be as meaningless as blaming the buzzard for swooping down on the dove.'

From these academic expressions of racist thinking with their emphasis on morality as the product of the 'race-soul' and on the unbridgeable gulf between the major racial groups—Hitler's three-fold classification in *Mein Kampf* differentiated sharply between: (i) culture-creators (i.e. Aryans), (ii) culture-carriers (Chinese, etc.) and (iii) culture-destroyers (i.e. Jews)—it was a relatively short step to statements such as these: 'Whatever Nordic man has in common with non-Aryans, he also has in common with the lower apes'; and, 'To those who say Jews are also human beings we say that bugs are animals too, but animals that have to be destroyed. After all no one claims that there are decent fleas and bugs, one just kills the lot.'

Conditioning the Germans to accept such theories, and the practices arising out of them, required the re-shaping of the thought processes and emotional reflexes of a whole nation. A typical example is the way in which people's reaction to the weak who would normally become objects of pity was manipulated. (It should be noted here that the Nazi mind reacted to weakness in an opponent with increased—rather than diminished—hatred. This applied to the Jews, to the Weimar regime and also to Britain; whereas Hitler's early writings contained respectful references to Britain, his attitude to her during the era of appeasement became one of vicious antagonism mingled with derision.) To counteract any stirrings of compassion for the Jews, the Nazis employed the following rationalisation:

'The apparent powerlessness of our opponents is only further proof of their cunning. The fact that they lack any overt means of harming us is only additional evidence of their secret power to place us in deadly peril.' The more violent the acts of persecution, the greater became the need to justify them by believing ever more strongly in the victims' guilt. In this manner was set in motion the vicious circle of lie-engendered violence known as the Final Solution.

The Final Solution, the killing of the 'incurably' ill, the shooting of hostages, the slave-labour programme, all these required the active co-operation of no more than a fraction of the German population, but they also needed the acquiescence of the great majority. That this passive assent was forthcoming was in no small measure due to the operation of such simple pressures as the spying of children on their parents, the obligatory use of the Hitler salute in all social intercourse and the occasional arrest of people for breaking laws not yet in force at the time of the offence. The first meant that if a non-Nazi wanted peace and filial respect, he had to do violence to his own feelings, even in the sanctity of his home; the obligation to say *Heil Hitler* countless times each day implied saying one thing and thinking another. And the ever-present possibility of imprisonment on unspecified charges put people in a position in which they always tried to anticipate what the Nazi state would demand of them next. Doing violence to one's own feelings, saying one thing and believing another and always thinking one jump ahead of the dictatorship's next move, are all designed to take a heavy toll of mental energy and can eventually destroy a person's belief in himself. To avoid this breakdown, most non-Nazi Germans eventually did this: they changed their own feelings so that they need no longer do violence to them; thought inwardly what they had to say publicly; and made the regime's mentality so much their own that the need for keeping one step ahead no longer arose.

We now turn from a consideration of the Nazi regime's successes to one of its failures. Of these failures the ultimate outcome of World War II is, of course, the most obvious. Contributory to this defeat were two weaknesses in the German war effort which arose directly out of the self-defeating application of rigid Nazi dogma. The first is connected with German inactivity in the nuclear field, a vital omission directly attributable to the Nazi ban on pursuing research into Jewish, i.e. Einsteinian, physics.

The second concerns the fact that the total mobilisation of German women for the industrial war effort was too long delayed to be of very much use. This delay resulted from Hitler's view of woman as primarily a child-bearing, kitchen-minded creature.

The *Führerprinzip*—'absolute authority of every leader over those below him and absolute responsibility of every leader to those above him'—was another source of Nazi weakness. Suspicious of Party bosses powerful enough to be potential rivals Hitler tended to play off his chief lieutenants against each other. Some of these men had been so adroit in 'empire building' that three vast rival political machines existed in Germany by the time war broke out: the government and civil service (under Goering), the Party apparatus (headed by Bormann after Hess's flight), and thirdly the SS (led by Himmler). This tangle of competing authorities produced remarkable instances of mismanagement. At the height of the war in pursuance of two contradictory directives thousands of Volksdeutsche were being repatriated into the Reich to make the area of German settlement more compact, whilst Reich-Germans were sent into eastern Europe to establish colonies among the Slav subject-peoples. The treatment of the largest of the Slav inferior races, the Russians, afforded another instance of Nazi leaders at cross-purposes. Rosenberg, the Minister for the Occupied East, had devised a scheme for surrounding Russia proper by a chain of Nazi-satellite states such as the Baltic and

Caucasian Republics, the Ukraine, etc. This scheme which would
have split the peoples of the USSR into Russians and non-Russians
was made inoperative by the atrocities of the SS and the deportation of slave workers—factors which greatly promoted the growth
of united Soviet patriotism.

The closing phase of the war witnessed, in addition to Himmler's
and Goering's 'treasonable' conduct towards Hitler, an open
divergence of purpose inside the Nazi leadership. Whilst the
apostles of total destruction, such as the nihilistic Goebbels, aimed
to plunge the whole of Germany into chaos, the more sober-
minded technocrats, such as Armaments Minister Speer, were
taking steps to ensure the continuity of national life, even in
defeat.

At a time when Speer's thoughts were already beginning to
turn to the problems of Germany's continued existence after defeat,
Hitler and Bormann were still working out plans for the conduct
of German affairs after victory. A consideration uppermost in
their minds was the fall in the birth-rate resulting from the heavy
casualties incurred in the war. To offset this 'grave deficiency in
the hereditary substance of the German people', it was planned to
legalise bigamy in the post-war Third Reich. All unmarried
women who had reached the age of thirty would have to become
the second wives of certain selected types of male whose increased
propagation the state thought desirable. (These included all Party
functionaries as well as war veterans decorated for bravery in
battle.) Fears that the clergy might inspire widespread opposition
to the introduction of this scheme were brushed aside—the
success of Himmler's *Lebensborn* institutions where unmarried
mothers could have their children brought up at the public
charge being adduced as proof of the German public's readiness
to discard outworn concepts of morality.

Other Nazi post-war plans dealt in detail with the colonisation
of the vast spaces of eastern Europe where, according to Hitler,
Germany's future destiny lay. The problem of the millions of
Russians and Poles inhabiting those areas was to be tackled along
three lines:

(a) Slavs who had pronounced Aryan characteristics were to
be Germanised.

(b) Those whose racial tests were 'negative' but who could be employed as helots were to be kept alive; their numbers were, however, to be steadily reduced by over-work, lack of medical care, food-shortages, etc.

(c) The rest—the rebellious, intelligent, 'work-shy', or simply too numerous ones—would be liquidated.

The victory of the Third Reich would thus have resulted, in addition to the 35,000,000 to 40,000,000 casualties of the Second World War, in annually recurring massacres of further millions. The Nazi regime would gradually have been extended across the globe and mankind would have become unalterably divided into masters and slaves, subjects or objects of permanent exploitation. The full implications of such a system are enshrined in these calculations an SS official submitted to his superiors, an example of Nazism rendering account:

'The hiring out of concentration camp inmates to industrial enterprises yields an average daily return of six to eight marks from which 70 pfennigs must be deducted for food and clothing. Assuming a camp inmate's life expectancy of nine months, we multiply this sum by 270: the total is 1,431 marks. This profit can be increased by rational utilisation of the corpse, i.e. by means of gold fillings, clothing, valuables, etc., but on the other hand every corpse represents a loss of two marks, which is the cost of cremation.'

Bibliography

GENERAL HISTORY

Buchheim, Hans, *The Third Reich*, 1961.
Bullock, Alan, *Hitler, A Study in Tyranny*, 1952.
Eyck, Erich, *History of the Weimar Republic*, 1962.
Jarman, T. L., *The Rise and Fall of Nazi Germany*, 1955.
Mau, H., & Krausnick, H., *German History 1933–1945*, 1959.
Shirer, William, *The Rise and Fall of the Third Reich*, 1960.
Taylor, A. J. P., *The Course of German History*, 1945.
Wheeler-Bennett, J., *The Nemesis of Power*, 1953.

FOREIGN POLICY

Gilbert, M., & Gott, R., *The Appeasers*, 1963.
Namier, Lewis B., *In the Nazi Era*, 1952.
Wiskemann, Elizabeth, *The Rome-Berlin Axis*, 1949.

BIOGRAPHY

Jetzinger, Franz, *Hitler's Youth*, 1958.
Heiber, Helmut, *Adolf Hitler*, 1961.
Hitler, Adolf, *Mein Kampf* (unexpurgated edition, 1939).
Hitler's Table Talk, 1953.
Manvell, R., & Fraenkel, H., *Doctor Göbbels*, 1960.
  Hermann Göring, 1962.
Trevor-Roper, H. R., *The Last Days of Hitler*, 1947.

RESISTANCE

Rothfels, Hans, *The German Opposition to Hitler*, 1960.

OCCUPATION

Reitlinger, Gerald, *The House Built on Sand*, 1960.

ANTISEMITISM

Reichmann, Eva, *Hostages of Civilisation*, 1950.

TERROR

Crankshaw, Edward, *Gestapo*, 1956.
Kogon, Eugen, *The Theory and Practice of Hell*, 1950.
Reitlinger, Gerald, *The SS—Alibi of a Nation*, 1956.

GENOCIDE

Hilberg, Raul, *The Destruction of European Jewry* (Chicago, 1961).
Reitlinger, Gerald, *The Final Solution*, 1953.

DIARIES, EYE-WITNESS ACCOUNTS

Frank, Anne, *The Diary of a Young Girl*, 1952.
Hersey, John. *The Wall*, 1950.
Levi, Primo, *If This is a Man*, 1959.
Presser, Jakob, *The Breaking Point* (New York, 1958).

Index